JUICES & SMOOTHIES

JUICES & SMOOTHIES

LUCY DONCASTER

170 fresh nutrition-packed recipes for health, detox and energy

LORENZ BOOKS

2

Contents

Juicing for health

10 minutes to change your life. That's all it takes to make a healthy juice or shake-style drink, yet this very small and simple step can have a massive impact on your health and well-being.

Introducing a healthy juice or shake a day is an easy way to boost nutrition levels, making you feel and look good, not just in the short term but as an easily maintained long-term lifestyle choice. We are told we should all be eating at least five portions of vegetables and fruit a day but the reality is we should be aiming for seven to eight, and some recent advice recommends five portions of vegetables and two of fruit a day. These two food groups are at the core of the healthiest diets, and starting the day with a juice or shake is a great way to boost your intake. Enjoy foods as nature intended, avoiding refined processed products, artificial chemical sweeteners, flavourings and preservatives. If you can, replace them with foods that have been grown locally in a sustainable and environmentally friendly way.

When your body feels good, you feel good. If you eat a diet of junk food, processed carbs and fizzy drinks you will feel sluggish, your skin will lose its vitality and if you are not already piling on the pounds, you very soon will be. With levels of obesity, type 2 diabetes, heart disease and cancer rising, it makes sense to look at what you eat.

How often do you skip breakfast because you don't have time, or refuel at your desk with a hurried sandwich. Do you sit at the table in the evening and enjoy the food you eat, or mindlessly munch on the sofa in front of the TV? We can all say we are too tired, too stressed, too busy to shop and buy healthy options, but don't wait any longer to start making changes.

Other factors such as age, build, lifestyle and activity levels also affect our health. The old adage of a little of what you fancy does you good still rings true, it's just that we don't tend to eat little bits any more. The key to maintaining a healthy diet is to enjoy your food and to eat a wide range, in moderation. So, say yes to juices and smoothies but not in place of all meals: use a drink as one meal a day or as a healthy snack, perhaps drinking up to two a day to boost weight loss or aid a detox diet for a few days.

For optimum health, aim to include foods from the main groups of protein, good fats and complex carbs. Try to be as healthy as you can – you don't have to ban cake or biscuits altogether, just eat them in moderation. You will have the odd bad day, but think of the week as a whole and once you embrace a healthier way of eating you will find that you crave chips, cake and chocolate less. Alternatively, swap them for one of the indulgent shakes and slushes in this book, which contain some healthy ingredients, though they are a treat as some contain natural fat and sugar.

The vast majority of the juices and smoothies in this book are packed with nutrient-dense vegetables, fruits, nuts and seeds. They are rich in antioxidants and phytochemicals that can boost immunity, help protect us against cancers, and reduce the risk of cardiovascular disease, strokes, diabetes and obesity. If you don't have a particular ingredient, mix and match with something that you do have. The recipes can be flexible. Don't have any kale? Add a handful of spinach instead. No almond milk? Swap in rice, oat or soya milk. The aim is to help you to produce a wide range of delicious, nutritious and appealing drinks for different scenarios, from sustaining breakfast shakes to superfood juice shots. Good health!

What makes up a healthy diet?

We need each of the main food groups to keep our body in tip-top shape, and drinking a healthy smoothie, shake or juice is an easy way to do this. Here's the low-down on each of the groups and advice on how to include them in your daily diet.

Protein

This is essential for our body, for growth, repair and maintenance of cells everywhere from our muscles and bones to our hair and fingernails. It helps create enzymes that aid digestion, and produces antibodies that fight off infection and hormones that keep our body working properly.

Proteins are broken down during digestion into amino acids. There are 20 in total, but only eight can be obtained from food; the rest can be made by the body. However, proteins cannot be stored in the body. And, if you don't have enough fats or carbs in your diet, proteins will instead be broken down and used as energy. If you do a lot of exercise or are vegan, it may be a good idea to boost protein levels by adding nuts, protein powders, soya milk, yogurt or tofu to your drinks.

PROTEIN-PACKED HEMP

Hemp makes a great addition to any juice or smoothie as it is one of the few plants that contains all 20 amino acids. It is also rich in essential fatty acids omega 6 and 3 and is a good source of vitamin E. Use it in powdered form or as a cold-pressed oil. Stir a little into a juice or add to a shake before blending.

Good carbs

Carbohydrates often get a bad press, yet we need them for energy, rather like a car needs fuel to run. Just like fuel, there are different grades:

Empty carbs – refined white sugars and flours give the body a quick energy boost followed by a low-energy dip, and leave us feeling sluggish. Usually found in cakes and pastries that are high in fats with little other nutrient benefit, it is this kind of carbs that gives the food group a bad name.

Complex carbs – these are the good guys. They include wholegrain flours, cereals, oats, barley, seeds, vegetables and fruit. As they take longer to digest, they leave us feeling fuller for longer and give out a slowly released energy boost that helps to maintain blood sugar levels, aids concentration, and reduces fatigue. They are rich in vitamins and minerals, and the high levels of fibre help maintain a healthy digestive system and reduce cholesterol.

Right It's easy to include many of the food groups in your juices, shakes and smoothies.

OATYLICIOUS

Just 15ml/1 tbsp uncooked wholegrain rolled oats added to a shake-style smoothie equals one of the three daily recommended portions of wholegrains. The risk of heart disease, stroke and type 2 diabetes may be up to 30 per cent lower in people who regularly eat wholegrains as part of a low-fat healthy lifestyle. Yet about 95 per cent of people don't eat enough wholegrains and, rather staggeringly, one in three eat none at all.

Are you too sweet?

It is feared by some health professionals that high levels of sugar in our diet may become as great a problem as alcohol consumption. Our generation consumes three times the amount of fructose than was the norm 50 years ago. Indeed, most of us have become very used to sweet things, which means that when you first begin to juice and blend healthy vegetable shakes you may feel the need to add a little extra sweetness. Fruits vary in their natural sweetness, so if a juice tastes a little sharp you may prefer to substitute an ingredient with something that is a little sweeter next time, perhaps adding a kiwi fruit instead of celery or fennel. For drinks that contain strong-tasting cabbage, spring greens or kale, you may like to drizzle up to a teaspoon of clear honey, maple syrup or agave syrup into the drink at the end. You might also try adding a little powdered palm or coconut sugar or lacuma powder. Avoid the powdered sugar substitutes – the low-calorie kind you add to tea or coffee – since these can be strong-tasting and overwhelm the natural flavours of a healthy juice or shake. They also somehow don't sit with the wholefood ethos of natural juices and shakes.

Being aware of the amounts of sugar that you consume in foods is key. Only then can you start to reduce the amounts of sugar in your diet. The average adult should have around 260g/9¼oz of carbohydrates a day, of which a maximum 90g/3½oz should be obtained from sugars. Ideally, we should be aiming to reduce this down to about seven teaspoons a day – this includes sugar already in foods and drinks. The good news is that as your palate begins to adjust to a new healthy way of eating and drinking you will find that you no longer crave very sweet things.

Left Clockwise from top left: Clear honey, maple, date and agave syrups and lacuma powder.

Above Packed with vitamins and minerals, dark green leafy veg are a great addition to drinks.

Healthy fats

Weight for weight, fats contain more than twice the amount of calories as carbohydrates or protein. Yet we need fat as a necessary part of every cell to help absorb fat-soluble vitamins A, D, E and K, to provide essential fatty acids and as a concentrated form of energy. The important thing is to consume the right kind of fats and in the right proportion. Adding half an avocado or a small drizzle of cold-pressed avocado, hemp or almond oil can be a great way to boost energy levels in smoothies and juices, using mono- or polyunsaturated fats rather than saturated ones.

Vitamins

Vegetables and fruits are rich in these complex substances, which are key for good health. Many chemical reactions cannot take place in the body without them; they are vital catalysts. B vitamins, for instance, are needed for the release of energy and for healthy nerve and muscle function. Beta-carotene, vitamin C and vitamin E are antioxidants and they act like a natural bodyguard to help fight free-radical damage, help protect against cancer and heart disease, and also reduce the risk of age-related diseases such as cataracts, Alzheimer's and Parkinson's disease.

Minerals

The minerals manganese, zinc, selenium and copper are part of the team of antioxidants that help prevent free-radical damage. Minerals also help regulate bodily fluids, make enzymes, and are involved in metabolic processes. Just a handful of dark green leafy vegetables or a tablespoon of dried sea vegetables is all it takes to boost our daily multi-mineral intake, while avocados add a manganese boost, bananas add potassium and nuts add selenium.

Liquid refreshment

All smoothies and shakes require liquid to be added to the mix of fruit, vegetables, nuts and seeds. You can choose from regular dairy milk, unsweetened nut, seed, pea, soya, rice and oat milk, coconut milk, coconut water, fruit juices or mineral water – the choice is very much yours. While certain liquids have been specified throughout this book, do swap them if you prefer.

Keep hydrated

Drinking water is key to staying healthy. If you don't drink enough you can become tired, have poor concentration and headaches, and may feel light-headed. You may also suffer constipation, kidney stones and urinary tract infections.

In general, women should aim for at least 1.6 litres/2½ pints per day, while men need 2 litres/3½ pints. Age, gender, build, lifestyle, activity and the weather also affect how much we need to drink. It sounds a lot, but if you keep a glass of water on your desk at work and always have water on the table at meal times, it is achievable. Tea, herbal tea and coffee also count, although don't overdo the tea or coffee as caffeine is a diuretic.

Milks

Dairy milk is extremely good for hydration, as well as being nutritious. In fact, it is better than water after sport since it stays in the body for longer, allowing more time for the water in it to be absorbed. Many recipes in this book include milk, sometimes in its full-fat or whole form and at others when it is semi-skimmed or skimmed.

Over the past few years, however, there has been a huge rise in popularity and availability of nut, seed, pea, soya, rice, oat and hemp milks. But why has this occurred? There are several reasons. More and more people are becoming vegan, or moving away from a diet rich in red meat and saturated fats towards a healthier plant-based diet that cuts down dairy as well as meat and fish. Some people feel that dairy milk makes them feel bloated or that it adds to symptoms of indigestion, IBS, sinus problems or skin complaints, though only a small minority of people actually have a serious allergy to the milk sugar lactose and milk protein casein. Others just prefer the taste. Unless you have a dairy intolerance or allergy, use whichever you prefer.

If you do choose to buy non-dairy milks, read the labels and go for ones that are unsweetened and that have been fortified with calcium and vitamin D. Some brands will also have added vitamin B12, a vitamin that is difficult to obtain on a vegan diet.

Soya milk – this has the strongest taste and contains more protein than the other non-dairy milks; it also contains vitamins A, D and B12, plus potassium. It is usually fortified with calcium.

Almond milk – lower in calories than soya milk, this is more like cow's milk in texture. It is free from cholesterol, saturated fat and lactose. Even though almonds are a good source of protein, almond milk is not, but it does contain vitamins A and D. Buy it fortified with calcium.

Rice milk – this thin milk is the least allergenic of all the non-dairy milks. It is high in carbohydrates but contains almost no protein. During processing, the carbs change to sugars, giving it a natural sweetness. Buy it fortified with calcium.

Oat milk – made with oats, water and salt, this also has a thinner texture. It is a good source of fibre and is one of the most eco-friendly milks.

Hemp milk – this can be a little grainy but is higher in heart-healthy omega 3 fatty acids than the other non-dairy milks.

MAKING YOUR OWN NUT MILKS

Although readily available in supermarkets you might also like to try making your own nut milks at home.

1 Add 125g/4½oz/1 cup roughly chopped unblanched almonds (with brown skins) or other nuts to a large plastic container and cover with 1 litre/1¾ pints/4 cups cold filtered water. Cover and leave to soak overnight.

2 Transfer the nuts and the soaking liquid to a blender, in batches if needed, and blitz until as smooth as possible.

3 Strain the liquid through a sieve or strainer lined with muslin or cheesecloth into a jug or pitcher. You should now have about 1 litre/1¾ pints of nut milk.

4 Pour the strained liquid into a bottle, seal and keep it in the fridge up to 2 days. If it separates, simply stir it before use.

5 The remaining nut meal can be kept and a tablespoon or two added to shakes or smoothie-style drinks, or you can use it instead of or as part of the pulp for making crackers (see page 27).

Eat a rainbow

Fruit and vegetables come in an amazing array of colours and sizes. Eating a wide variety of these foods is the key to a healthy diet, and what better way to include them than making a daily juice or smoothie.

Health professionals recommend that we eat at least five portions of vegetables and fruit a day, with some suggesting that we should be ideally aiming for seven to eight portions. Despite this, many of us don't even manage three or four. This needs to change. Rich in cancer-protecting antioxidants, many of which give the fruit and vegetables their deep colours, as well as vitamins, minerals, carbs and fibre, this huge food group can also help to protect against heart disease, obesity and diabetes.

Happily, one easy way to boost your fruit and vegetable intake is to transform them into juices, smoothies, smoothie bowls and even milkshakes. And the good news doesn't stop there. There are countless different blends to choose from, so consuming these foods will never be boring!

Green

Broccoli – the darker the florets, irrespective of colour, the higher the amounts of vitamin C and beta-carotene, which the body converts into vitamin A. Broccoli also contains beneficial indoles – the nitrogen compounds that may help protect DNA from damage and so protect against cancer.

Cabbage, collard greens and spring greens – these are all rich in vitamin C, E and K, plus folates required for cell division and the formation of DNA, along with potassium for fluid balance and to help regulate blood pressure. They also contain indoles. Use cabbage sparingly in drinks as the flavour can be a little overpowering.

Above It's so important to eat a rainbow! By including a wide range of raw vegetables and fruits in your diet, you will help to keep your body in tip-top shape and fight off disease.

Herbs – choose from parsley, coriander/cilantro, mint and basil for a chlorophyll-boosting, detoxing addition to juices and smoothies. Parsley contains useful amounts of vitamin C and iron and can help as a breath freshener, while mint aids digestion and also freshens breath. Coriander aids digestion and adds a spicy, fresh tang to any drinks. Basil acts as a natural tranquilizer and is thought by herbalists to calm the nervous system, aid digestion and ease stomach cramps.

Lettuce – choose darker green leaves for the most nutritional value. As the leaves have such a high water content, they are hydrating and calories are low. Amounts of vitamin C and K vary between types of lettuce, with romaine lettuce having some of the highest.

Kale – like broccoli, whatever the variety, the darker the leaves the higher the amounts of vitamin C they contain. Kale also has vitamin B and K, chlorophyll and iron, which helps with the oxygenation and health of blood cells, so helping to fight fatigue. It also contains the antioxidant lutein, which may help to protect against macular eye degeneration; indoles, which may protect against oestrogen-related cancers; and sulforaphane, which helps the liver to detoxify carcinogenic compounds. Buy as whole leaves or bags of ready-shredded to save time.

Sea vegetables – seaweed is packed with nutrition. It is rich in iodine, needed for normal functioning of the thyroid gland, with smaller amounts of copper and iron for healthy blood, magnesium for proper functioning of muscles and nerves, calcium for healthy bones, potassium for the balance of fluids, and zinc for the body's immune system.

Seaweed can be bought dried and ready-shredded in small packs – look for mixed sea vegetables that include dulce, nori and sea lettuce. There is no need to soak this in water before use – simply add a spoonful to a smoothie or smoothie bowl when blending.

Spinach – this is packed with a high concentration of carotenoids, including beta-carotene and lutein, which may help protect against cancer. It also contains potassium and folates. Choose baby spinach leaves as they are lower in oxalates; as the leaves grow in size so the amount of oxalates increases and this can inhibit the absorption of calcium and iron from the spinach. When added to smoothies, spinach blends to an ultra-smooth purée, and it can be juiced. It has a delicate flavour that doesn't overpower berries and other fruits. You might also like to try Swiss chard with their white stems or rainbow chard with their vibrant multicoloured stems.

Apples – choose apples for their natural energy-boosting sweetness. The pectin they contain helps to lower cholesterol and also to activate beneficial bacteria in the large intestine, while adding vitamin C and boosting fibre.
Avocado – thought to be one of the most nutritionally complete fruits, avocados are rich in concentrated energy in the form of mono-unsaturated fats, plus vitamin B6, which is needed to aid energy release. They are rich in potassium, which helps regulate blood pressure and lower the risk of heart attacks and strokes, and vitamin E, with smaller amounts of vitamin C and lutein to help protect against macular degeneration. Avocados add a velvety creaminess to smoothies and smoothie bowls; try drizzling a little avocado oil over the top, too, for an added boost.
Green grapes – fresh, tangy and a good source of potassium to help regulate blood pressure, grapes add a natural sweetness to drinks and contain only 60 calories per 100g/3¾oz.
Kiwi fruit – packed with immune-boosting vitamin C and a good source of potassium, kiwis also contain the antioxidant lutein, which may help to protect against macular degeneration. The little black seeds are a good source of soluble fibre, which can also help to lower blood cholesterol.

Yellow and orange

Carrots – these really do help you see in the dark, as the beta-carotene they contain is converted to vitamin A in the body, which helps our eyes adjust quickly to changes in light. In traditional medicine, carrots were known for their detoxifying properties. Their high levels of vitamin A are also thought to fight the signs of ageing.
Corn – these bright yellow kernels are naturally sweet and are packed with complex carbs and fibre for a slow-release energy boost.

Left Brightly coloured fruits and vegetables are crammed full of nutrients, all of which have different beneficial properties.

Sweet potatoes – this vegetable is naturally sweet and can be used in place of added sugar. It contains vitamins A and C, fibre and potassium, plus useful amounts of magnesium and manganese.
Yellow bell peppers – all peppers are rich in vitamin A, C and K. These vitamins help to prevent cell damage, cancer and diseases related to ageing.
Mango – this fruit is rich in energy-boosting fruit sugars plus beta-carotene and vitamin C.
Oranges, lemons, limes and grapefruit – these are all rich in vitamin C to help boost our immune system and to aid the absorption of iron. Pink grapefruit and blood oranges also contain good amounts of beta-carotene, while lemons contain limonene, a phytochemical that is thought to help protect against cancer.
Papaya – this soft fruit contains the enzyme papain, which can aid digestion. It is rich in vitamin C, plus beta-carotene with smaller amounts of calcium and iron.
Pineapple – full of natural sugars, vitamin C and the digestive enzyme bromelain, which can have a calming effect on the stomach. It is also thought to have anti-inflammatory properties.

Red

Cherries – rich in beta-carotenes and potassium, cherries have anti-inflammatory properties and may be beneficial for those with gout and arthritis.
Cranberries – famous for helping to prevent urinary tract infections, cranberries are rich in antioxidants and may help protect against cancer and heart disease. They may even help prevent mouth ulcers and have anti-ageing properties.
Goji berries – these tiny, bright red fruits are brimming with beta-carotene, and also contain vitamin C, antioxidants and fibre.
Tomatoes – these fruits are rich in lycopene, a carotenoid pigment that is thought to help prevent against some forms of cancer. Tomatoes are also a good source of potassium, with smaller amounts of vitamin A, C and E. They contain 90 per cent water so are also good for rehydration.

WHAT ARE ANTIOXIDANTS?

Antioxidants are one of the first lines of defence that the body uses in order to prevent free radicals, which occur during oxidation, from damaging cells. They also help repair any damage. This is important since DNA-containing cells that undergo oxidative stress have been linked to cancer, heart disease, stroke, Parkinson's, Alzheimer's and autoimmune diseases, as well as cognitive decline and macular degeneration.

There are many antioxidant compounds in fruit and vegetables but the most common dietary ones are beta-carotene, which is used by the body to make vitamin A, vitamin C and vitamin E; anthocyanins in blueberries; flavonoids found in tea, red wine and citrus fruits; indoles found in cruciferous vegetables such as broccoli, cabbage and cauliflower; lignans in seeds; lutein in leafy greens; and lycopene in tomatoes and pink grapefruit, along with minerals zinc, selenium and copper.

Raspberries – as well as being high in vitamin C, raspberries also contain manganese, which helps with the metabolism of carbs, proteins and cholesterol and aids bone health.
Strawberries – packed with more vitamin C than any other red berry, strawberries have great antiviral and antibacterial properties. Rich in beta-carotene, they also contain lignin, which may help reduce blood cholesterol. Naturally sweet, they boost energy.
Watermelon – with its high water content, juicy watermelon helps to rehydrate and plump your skin. It also contains the antioxidant glutathione, which is thought to help boost the immune system and fight infection. Like tomatoes, watermelon gets its colour from lycopene, which is believed to help prevent some types of cancer.

Purple

Beetroot – this has high sugar levels, which means it is great for boosting energy. It also contains folates, vitamin C and potassium, with small amounts of iron. The high levels of nitrates are thought to benefit sportspeople and may help slow the progression of dementia. Beetroot also contains the antioxidant group of betalains.
Blackberries – a good source of vitamin C, folates and fibre, blackberries also contain salicylates, a natural asprin-like compound.
Blueberries – packed with antioxidants called flavonoids, blueberries may help to protect against cancer, premature ageing, heart disease and degenerative diseases caused by oxidative stress. They are also rich in vitamin C, natural fruit sugars and pectin to help lower cholesterol, plus they act as an anti-inflammatory.
Plums – these are a good source of vitamin C, but don't eat too many as they can have a laxative effect.
Pomegranate – these red seeds are packed with fibre and contain vitamins A, C and E, plus iron.

White

Bananas – this is the only fruit that contains tryptophan, plus vitamin B6, which together help the body to produce serotonin, making it the natural good-mood food. Rich in fruit sugars and starch, bananas boost energy while the potassium they contain helps to regulate blood pressure.
Cauliflower – the sulphurous compounds found in cauliflower may help to protect against some cancers. It also contains vitamin C.
Pears – like apples, pears contain natural fruit sugars, which are absorbed more slowly by the body than refined sugars. Pears are also rich in pectin, which helps to lower cholesterol.

Right All of these red foods are naturally sweet and bring a cocktail of benefits to your drinks.

Nuts and seeds

Boost the protein and nutrient levels in your shakes, smoothies and smoothie bowls by adding a spoonful of nuts or seeds in butter or ground form (so they blend easily), or top a smoothie bowl with a sprinkling of these superfoods in their whole state.

Go nutty

Nuts provide most of the B vitamins, along with the minerals phosphorous, iron, copper and potassium. They are also one of the richest sources of vitamin E, although both vitamin E and thiamine are destroyed when nuts are roasted. Walnuts, peanuts and hazelnuts are especially rich in essential fatty acids, which are vital for normal tissue growth and development. Selenium can be a difficult mineral for a vegan person to obtain, but happily Brazil nuts are an excellent source.

Unfortunately the fat content of nuts does bump up the calories, so just eat them in moderation. Most varieties contain more than 550 calories per 100g/3¾oz, but by adding just a spoonful of nut or seed butter to your drink you'll be more easily able to restrict your intake than you would if you were to eat them from a bowl. Homemade butters are best, since you can control how much sugar and salt, if any, that you add. If you buy nut butter, choose brands that do not have added sugar and only the minimum of salt.

Left Clockwise from top right: cashew nuts, pecan nuts, walnuts, pistachio nuts, almonds, hazelnuts, Brazil nuts and toasted coconut (technically not a nut, but a fruit).

Note: If making a drink for someone else, check they don't have a nut or peanut allergy. Do not give whole nuts or seeds to children under five. Supervize older children to avoid any risk of choking.

The mighty seed

Seeds are cheap, easy to find and add extra nutritional value to any smoothie or shake. They make a great protein booster for those who do not eat meat, and are high in fibre, although be aware that they are high in calories: 1 tablespoon can contain up to 100 calories. However, this is derived from the unsaturated or good fat that they contain, making them a valuable source of energy.

Pumpkin seeds – these contain iron for healthy blood, magnesium for healthy cells, and zinc for normal growth and development.

Sunflower seeds – used to make oil and margarine as well as seed butter or simply eaten raw, these contain useful amounts of vitamin C and are high in linoleic acid, which is needed for the maintenance of cell membranes.

Sesame seeds – these contain vitamin E and calcium. They're delicious sprinkled over a smoothie bowl.

Flaxseeds/linseeds – these can be bought as brown or golden seeds. They are one of the best food sources of lignans, which are rich in antioxidants and act as phytoestrogens, which help balance hormone levels. They also contain omega 3 and 6 essential fatty acids, plus magnesium, manganese, vitamin B and fibre. Buy them ready ground or grind your own so that the body can absorb the nutrients that they contain. As these seeds have such tough outer walls, if you leave them whole they will just pass right through the body adding only roughage to the diet.

Chia seeds – these tiny seeds contain protein, fibre, omega 3, 6 and 9 fatty acids plus calcium, iron, copper and zinc. When mixed with liquid they form a gel, so serve any drink that contains them immediately. Alternatively, stir in a little extra liquid to loosen just before serving.

Above Clockwise from top left: hulled hemp seeds, sunflower seeds, pumpkin seeds, chia seeds, sesame seeds (centre), flaxseeds and ground flaxseeds.

Hemp seeds – rich in essential fatty acids, made up of two-thirds of omega 6 and one-third of omega 3 fatty acids, hemp contains all 20 amino acids, including the essential ones required for boosting protein for those on a vegan diet. In addition, they contain B vitamins, vitamin E, carotene, calcium and magnesium. Buy them as hulled seeds as these are easier for the body to digest and extract the important nutrients from, as oil, or as a fine green powder (see page 8 for more information about hemp powder).

Nutrient boosters

Visit any good health food store and you will find a range of unusual nutrient-boosting powders that you can add to drinks. If you are not familiar with them, here is a run-down.

Spirulina – this dark blue-green powder is made from dried algae and contains 60 per cent protein, vitamin B12 – a difficult vitamin for those on a vegan diet to obtain – plus essential fatty acids. It is also thought to have immune-boosting properties and may help normalize blood pressure.
Chlorella – this is also a dark green powdered algae, but unlike spirulina it has a hard cell wall that needs to be broken down during manufacture so that the body can absorb it during digestion.
Hemp powder – this is another green powder and, like spirulina, is packed with protein. In fact, it is one of only a few plants to contain all amino acids, as well as being rich in essential fatty acids omega 6 and 3 and a good source of vitamin E. It can also be bought as hemp oil or hulled seeds.
Wheatgrass – this can be bought in powdered form or as grass sold in trays. As only a small amount is used at a time, powdered wheatgrass makes a handy store-cupboard nutrient booster. It contains all eight essential amino acids needed by the body for growth and repair of all cells, plus B vitamins, vitamins C, E and K, and iron.

Matcha – sold in concentrated powdered form, this green tea contains 137 times the amount of antioxidants than the same weight of regular green tea. Buy in teabags and soak in boiled water in the same way you would any other herbal tea.
Moringa – this green powder is derived from the dried leaves of the native Indian moringa tree and has long been used in traditional Indian medicine for its antibacterial properties and as a digestive aid. Moringa contains all essential amino acids plus it is rich in vitamins A, B, E and the minerals magnesium, potassium and calcium, as well as small amounts of iron.
Açaí – these little berries can be found in the Amazon rainforest. The raw fruit is hard to buy since it goes rancid quickly after picking, so buy it as sachets of freeze-dried powdered fruit and sprinkle into smoothies or use as a decoration. Rich in antioxidants, healthy omega fatty acids and fibre, it can also be bought as frozen purée.
Baobab – this white powder comes from a dried coconut-sized fruit from Africa. Rich in potassium, calcium, vitamin C, antioxidants and small amounts of iron, it is thought to aid digestion and enhance the growth of probiotic bacteria in the gut.
Raw cacao – this is made by cold-pressing unroasted cocoa beans, removing the fat but retaining important antioxidants, minerals and the amino acid tryptophan, which aids relaxation and sleep. The cocoa powder used in baking is darker in colour as it has been roasted at high temperatures, lowering the nutritional value and giving it a stronger, slightly bitter taste.

Left Açaí powder is high in antioxidants and fibre.

Sports nutrition

Juices and smoothies are great choices both before and after exercise, being packed with energy and nutrients and quick to make – which is essential if you if you are to recover properly following an intense workout. They also, of course, help you to rehydrate.

There are all sorts of powders that you can add to drinks, often to boost protein levels or to provide other sport-specific benefits, including protein-rich spirulina and hemp powder, described already. Here are some of the best:

Protein powder – this is usually a pre-mixed product made from protein-rich plants, such as soya, hemp, chickpeas, peas or rice, or a mixture, combined with fibre and added vitamins and minerals. It is often flavoured – vanilla, chocolate and strawberry are popular – and is generally intended to be blended with some type of milk to make a flavoured shake. However, it can also be blended into smoothies and shakes containing other ingredients, so long as the flavours complement each other. For instance, you could add a scoop of vanilla or chocolate powder to a banana and nut butter milkshake, but you may think twice about adding strawberry powder to a green smoothie.

It is worth shopping around and paying close attention to the ingredients lists as products do vary in quality, and it pays to try before you buy in bulk as some are delicious while others are less pleasant. Also, do bear in mind that these powders are generally quite calorific, so they are best reserved for times when you are about to do or have just finished a workout. Just add a tablespoon to your drink before blending, rather than a large scoop.

Activated whey powder – often associated with bodybuilders, whey powder is a fantastic source of plant-based protein and in its activated form it is readily absorbed by the body. Read the packaging and use it in accordance with your exercise levels.

Above Clockwise from top left: wheatgrass powder, matcha teabags, baobab powder and spirulina.

Other forms of protein – hemp, pea, flax and rice powders are all packed with protein, as is egg white protein. As with the other powders, simply follow the instructions on the packaging regarding dosage and add the measured amount to your drink before you blend it. Hemp and pea powders have a more pronounced taste than the others, so they work best in combination with strongly flavoured ingredients.

L-glutamine – this amino acid in powder form aids recovery and increases fat burning, among other things, meaning that it is a great addition to a post-workout shake. Note: this powder is only really beneficial if you lead a very active lifestyle, since under normal conditions your body produces enough L-glutamine. However, if you do intense exercise you may deplete your natural stores, in which case it is useful to top up. Add just a small scoop, checking the packaging for the dosage.

Kitchen tips

Making juices and smoothies is really very simple, but there are some things you can do to maximize nutrition, make the most of the ingredients you use and avoid waste.

Making substitutions

Although the recipes in this book list specific vegetables, fruit, nuts, seeds and liquid, think of this as a starting point. If you don't have a particular ingredient, swap for something that you do have. If you don't have any coconut water, then just use ordinary water. Unsweetened nut milk can be interchanged with oat or rice milk – just make sure to choose unsweetened varieties. Soya milk has a slightly stronger flavour, so this is down to personal choice. Dairy yogurts can generally be swapped for dairy-free versions.

Almonds, cashew nuts and hazelnuts are all interchangeable. Brazil nuts may also be used but beware that you shouldn't eat more than about five per day as they are very high in selenium.

Seeds such as pumpkin, sesame, sunflower and flaxseeds are all interchangeable. The key to using them in drinks is to make sure they are finely ground. Either do this in the blender along with the other ingredients or grind small quantities of the ones that you use the most and keep in a small covered container in the fridge. Packs of ready-ground flaxseeds or mixed seeds are available but it is much cheaper to grind your own at home either in a liquidizer or spice mill.

Going organic

Once you have embraced the healthy eating ethos, buying organically grown vegetables, fruit, nuts, seeds and yogurt is a logical step, where you can, and is not much more expensive than regular produce. If you have a garden, why not grow your own? It is an easy, fun, satisfying and cheap way to eat organic produce.

Waste not want not

Fresh fruit can easily go soft in the fridge before you have a chance to use it all, which is wasteful and expensive. Don't bin it, though – just catch it before it has gone too far and use it to make your own freezer packs, or purée it and freeze it in ice cube trays. These are also great ways to preserve seasonal fruits for use later in the year when they are not available.

Homemade fruit freezer packs

Prepare the fruit as if you were eating it at once. Peel and pit mangoes and papaya. Cut the peel and core away from pineapple slices and then dice. Place the fruit on baking sheets and freeze, uncovered, until hard. Loosen the fruit then pack it into plastic bags. Press out the air, seal and label.

Bananas will only freeze for a maximum of 1 month; exotic fruits such as mangoes, papaya and pineapples up to 3 months; and summer berry fruits up to 6 months.

Homemade fruit ice cubes

Prepare individual fruits (not bananas – freeze those in peeled slices) as for fruit freezer packs, then blitz in a blender without sugar. Depending on the fruit's water content, you may need to add a little water to blend to a smooth purée.

Pour the purée into sections of an ice cube tray. Freeze until firm then turn out and pack each fruit type in different freezer bags. Squeeze out the air, then seal and label.

Each ice cube is about 10ml/2 tsp of purée. Take out as many as you need and defrost at room temperature or microwave briefly until soft.

Left Rather than throwing away the pulp that remains when you make a juice, consider whether you can use it for something else.

Get creative with pulp

Although you will have extracted much of the flavour and nutrition from the fruit and vegetables you use to make juices, some does remain in the pulp. It is also packed with fibre. So, instead of just throwing it away, scrape it into a bowl or, if you don't have time to use it immediately, into an airtight container and store it in the fridge until you do have more time. When you are ready, try one of these ideas to really get the full value from your ingredients:

1 If you have made a green smoothie that doesn't contain much fruit, you can easily make a light stock by putting the pulp in a pan and covering it with water, to come to about 5cm/2in above the level of the pulp. Simmer this mixture for about 20 minutes, or longer if you want a more intense stock, then pour it through a very fine sieve or strainer into a large heatproof jug. If the mesh on your strainer isn't fine enough to catch all the bits, you could line it with a piece of muslin or cheesecloth. However, it doesn't really matter if a few pieces of pulp filter through to the stock, unless you do need it to be perfectly clear.

This light stock is now ideal for using to make all sorts of soups – especially Asian ones if you included ginger in the juice. It can also be used in casseroles and stews, though do be aware that it won't have such an intense flavour as regular stock. Whatever you use it for, try to match the flavours you used in the juice to the dish. For instance, a stock made with carrot, ginger, turmeric and orange would be ideal for a carrot or squash soup, but perhaps less tasty in a broccoli and stilton soup or chicken stew.

If you don't want to use the stock immediately, leave it to cool, then either chill it and use it within 2 days, or freeze it, in one batch or as individual portions in an ice-cube tray.

2 You can also use the pulp to make some tasty crackers. The flavour of these will obviously depend on the ingredients you used in the juice. They are perhaps best made with pulp that mostly consists of vegetables, although a little sweetness is not unpleasant. See opposite for a base recipe, but do play around and try using different flavourings depending on the ingredients and your preferences. For instance, adding a pinch of curry powder, ground turmeric or cumin, dried chilli flakes, sea salt flakes, or sesame or poppy seeds will all produce interesting results. These are not especially crisp crackers, instead having a pleasingly chewy texture. They taste delicious as an accompaniment to a soup or casserole (made with pulp stock!), or spread with some hummus, soft cheese, butter or spread.

3 Depending on the composition of the juice pulp, it can be added to cakes – especially ones made with vegetables, such as carrot, parsnip or beetroot – bread and porridge, where it will bring added roughage, colour and flavour to the dish. As when making stock, think about what ingredients are in the pulp and what the best use is for the mixture. Chilli and red pepper would be delicious in cornbread but perhaps less welcome in your porridge!

4 If you don't have time or don't want to cook with the pulp, you can of course just compost it – either in a garden compost heap or the food waste you put out with your bins if that's available. However, if you have a dog, you may be able to give them a health boost while you enjoy your juice. Simply put a small amount of the pulp in their bowl and see if they like it. Note: It's really important to check that you only give your dog pulp made from ingredients that are safe for them to eat. Check online for the definitive list, but the general rule is that any fruit or vegetable that grows on a vine is toxic, so this rules out tomatoes, grapes, bell peppers and chillies. Alliums, rhubarb, nuts, caffeine, chocolate and avocados are also poisonous. However, green veg, carrots, cucumber, apples and pears are all safe, though try not to give them too much fruit as it is high in sugar, which isn't good for their teeth. Also, be aware that dogs strongly dislike citrus fruits, and some may also turn up their noses at ginger, fennel, celery and other strongly flavoured foods. If they refuse your offering, just compost it.

JUICE PULP CRACKERS

Makes about 16

175g/6oz/1 cup damp pulp left over from making a juice – preferably a green one

2.5ml/½ tsp baking powder

45ml/3 tbsp nutritional yeast flakes

30ml/2 tbsp ground flaxseeds

pinch of ground black pepper

30ml/2 tbsp olive oil

1 Preheat the oven to 150°C/300°F/Gas 2. Line a baking sheet with baking parchment or a silicone baking mat.

2 Put the juice pulp in a bowl and rub through it with your fingers, removing any large pieces of fruit or vegetable. You mostly want the finely shredded pulp. Sprinkle over the baking powder, nutritional yeast, flaxseeds and black pepper, then stir to mix with a spoon.

3 Drizzle over the olive oil and stir again to combine really well.

4 Transfer the mixture to the piece of baking parchment or the baking mat and use the back of the spoon and your fingers to squash it into a square about 6mm/¼in thick.

5 Use a blunt knife to cut the mixture into 16 roughly even squares. Using a palette knife, carefully separate the squares, shifting them apart on the baking paper or mat. You may need to re-form the square shapes and tidy the edges using the side of the knife.

6 Bake for 30–40 minutes, until slightly risen, fairly dry and light golden in colour.

7 Leave the crackers on the baking sheet for 5 minutes, then transfer to a wire rack and leave to cool completely. Store in an airtight container once cool, and eat within 2 days.

Getting equipped

For easy and successful juicing and smoothie-making you will need some specialist equipment. You probably already have a citrus juicer, but for juicing anything else you'll need a juicing machine. Here's a low-down on the different types to help you work out which is best for you.

Smoothie makers

A smoothie maker is a blender and, like all blenders, it is available with different jug or pitcher styles, motor sizes and price tags. So, how do you choose?

The Vitamix model has a large plastic blender goblet and lid that is easy to put together and, importantly, very easy to wash; simply add water and a drop of washing-up liquid and turn on the machine. The only downside is that it is tall so might not fit on the work surface under an overhead cupboard. With that powerful motor comes a hefty price tag, but if you like cooking and will use this ultra-durable blender for more than smoothies this may be the machine for you.

Mid-priced blenders look stylish and come in a variety of colours – even bright, bold primaries – as well as sleek black, glossy cream or white bases. Blender goblets vary in size and can be clear or made of ridged glass or plastic. Choose one that can crush ice so that you know the motor will be tough enough to give you a very smooth blend. Some machines may also come with a smoothie-style goblet with a screw top so that you can take your drink with you, plus a smaller goblet and different blade fittings for grinding nuts, seeds and coffee beans.

Nutribullet-style blenders are designed for just making individual portion-sized smoothies. Technically not a blender but an extractor, these are not much bigger than a water bottle. Easy to assemble, easy to use and very compact, they will fit on the work surface of even the smallest

Below Smoothie makers come in a range of sizes and powers, as well as pricepoints. Choose one that will meet your needs and fit your budget.

Right Juicers such as this centrifugal model work by shredding fruits and vegetables and then spinning out the juice from the pulp.

kitchen. Plus they are quick and easy to wash. Buy one that has several different-sized goblets, as well as two different blades – one for grinding nuts and seeds and the second for softer fruits – along with screw-on lids so that you simply add the lid to transport rather than decanting the drink into a second container. Some models also sell small insulated bags that just fit the blender goblet for drinks on the go. Always make sure to add liquid; even soft berries will require a splash of water, coconut water or milk to blend smooth.

Other models can make a good alternative to a Nutribullet. However, if it is too cheap it probably won't have a powerful enough motor to blend raw carrots, beetroot or whole seeds for a really smooth result, so bear in mind what kind of ingredients you will be likely be using. If you intend to mainly use avocado, berries, bananas, kale, spinach and ready-ground seeds then a cheaper model will be able to cope, but not harder roots or fine seeds. Also factor in how often you think you will be making a smoothie. If you are new to the idea, start with a cheaper model and upgrade when you get hooked.

Centrifugal juicers

These come in a variety of designs. They are the least expensive type of electric juicer, yet are adequate for most juices. They have a pulp collector into which the fibre and pulp residue is ejected. Some come with a jug attachment that collects the juice; others require a separate jug or glass to be placed under the spout. Centrifugal juicers finely grate vegetables and fruit and spin them at great speed, which separates the juice from the pulp. They are used to extract juice from hard vegetables and fruit, such as carrots and apples, and from leafy vegetables.

Masticating juicers

These are more hi-tech than centrifugal juicers, and also more expensive. Instead of shredding the produce they finely chop it and then force the pulp through a mesh to separate out the juice. Electric or manually operated, masticating juicers produce a greater volume of juice than centrifugal models and, because of the method of extraction, the juice contains more live enzymes. These are the best type for serious juice addicts.

WHAT ABOUT FOOD PROCESSORS?

While these can be used to make smoothies from soft ingredients, as well as slushes, they don't really blend mixtures containing harder ingredients – such as raw beetroot, carrot, apple, small seeds or nuts – finely enough to produce a smooth end result.

How to make juices

Juices are made by pressing vegetables and fruit through an electric juicer; as most of the fibre is removed, they rarely need any additional liquid to be added.

Although centrifugal and masticating juicers function in different ways, the preparation of fruits and vegetables, and the basic principles for using the machines, are much the same.

1 Always choose firm produce as soft fruits will not give successful results. For instance, firm, under-ripe pears work well, but soft, ripe pears are best prepared in a blender or food processor.

2 Most fruit and vegetables do not need to be cored or peeled since peel, pips, seeds and core will all be turned into pulp in the machine.

3 Given that the peel will be shredded, you should scrub any produce you are not going to peel with a hard brush under cold water to get rid of any dirt. If there is a waxy residue, use a little bit of soap or washing-up liquid to help dissolve this, then rinse the produce thoroughly.

4 Large pits of fruits such as peaches, nectarines and plums need to be removed. Cut round the middle of the fruit, using a small, sharp knife, then twist to break it into two halves. Carefully ease out the pit with the knife. Mangoes have a large, flat pit. Peel the fruit, cut the flesh away from either side of the pit, then remove as much flesh as possible from the pit.

5 All leafy vegetables, such as cabbages and lettuces, can be put through a juicer (1). Include the outer leaves, which are nutritionally superior, although these must be washed thoroughly first to remove any grit or dirt.

6 Citrus fruit can be put through a juicer. Ensure that you remove all the peel, but there is no need to remove the pips or pith.

7 When pushing the prepared produce through the feeder tube of the machine, it is very important that you use the plunger provided.

8 Put the ingredients through the machine in manageable quantities (2). Cut pears and apples into quarters, for example, and alternate them to ensure that the juices mix well. If you push too many or too-large pieces through, the machine will clog up. Remember to position a jug, pitcher or glass under the nozzle to catch the juice (3).

9 Push through a hard ingredient after softer ones, such as greens. This will keep the juice flowing freely and will prevent blockages. There should be little residue on the blades themselves (4).

CLEANING TIPS FOR JUICERS & BLENDERS

- Fill a sink with cold water and carefully take the equipment apart, following the manufacturer's instructions.
- Using a plastic spatula or spoon, scrape off any large pieces of residue.
- Plunge the non-electrical, removable parts into the cold water and leave them to soak until you are ready to clean them.
- Carefully scrub with a firm brush to loosen any residue. Rinse, then leave to air dry before reassembling the machine.

1

2

3

4

How to make smoothies

For those who prefer thick shakes or smoothie-style drinks a good blender is the way to go, and has the benefits of retaining the fibre contained within the ingredients.

Blenders and specialist smoothie makers work in fairly similar ways, and the preparation of fruit and veg is the same for both types of equipment.

1 Foods with inedible skins, such as bananas, mangoes and avocados, should be peeled. You can also simply scoop out avocado flesh from a halved avocado using a spoon (1). Fruits with edible skins, such as peaches or grapes, do not need to be peeled but should be washed. If you prefer a smoother texture, though, peel the fruits.

2 Fruits with large pits, cores or seeds, such as mangoes, plums, cherries and apples, should be pitted, cored or seeded.

3 Fruits with tiny seeds, such as raspberries, strawberries or kiwis, can be used whole, in which case the seeds add texture. However, if you prefer a smooth drink, the pulp can be pushed through a fine sieve or strainer, using a plastic spatula, to remove the seeds.

4 When using berries and currants, remove the stalks and leaves and wash the fruit thoroughly. An easy way to detach, or 'string', redcurrants, blackcurrants or whitecurrants from their stalks is to hold the bunch firmly at the top, then slowly draw the tines of a fork through the fruit so that the currants fall away.

5 Remove the hard central stem of any cabbage or other green leaves, if present, and dice the soft parts so they blend more easily. Soft greens such as spinach and lettuce give the smoothest results.

6 To properly blend ingredients in a blender or smoothie maker, it is important to add the liquid ingredients and the soft fruit or vegetables at the same time (2), then process everything together (3), otherwise the blades will not be able to blend the foods effectively. Serve immediately (4).

TROUBLESHOOTING

If you experience any problems using a juicer, blender or smoothie maker, or if the resulting drink is not quite what you imagined, the following may help:

The blend is too thick

Thin it using water or the juice of a watery fruit, or else add some dairy or non-dairy milk, yogurt or coconut water. To avoid muddling flavours, It is usually best to use more of the liquid stated in the recipe.

The blend is too pulpy

Strain the mixture through a sieve or strainer, pressing the pulp down with the back of a spoon. This is most likely to happen if you blend fibrous ingredients, such as dark leafy veg from which you didn't remove the core.

The ingredients get stuck to the side of the blender or smoothie maker

Stop blending and scrape down from the sides with a spatula before carrying on. This is important since it will ensure that all ingredients are mixed thoroughly.

1

2

3

4

How to make smoothie bowls

Smoothie bowls are thick fruit or fruit and vegetable mixtures that have been blended until smooth and soup-like. For ingredients that have a high water content there is no need to add extra liquid (as in this example, a strawberry and chia smoothie bowl). For others, top up with a little extra liquid, such as water, juice, a suitable type of milk, or coconut water from a carton.

Since you want the liquid to be thicker than it is for a smoothie that is drunk, you need to use a slightly different technique when making a smoothie bowl. Here are some tips:

- If your blender isn't very powerful, grind or finely chop the nuts and seeds on their own. You could make up your favourite mix and store it in a plastic container. Sprinkle it over the smoothie just before blending with liquid.
- Adding a mixture of fresh and frozen fruits will give the smoothie an ice cream-like texture.
- Don't overfill your blender goblet and always screw the lid on firmly. Begin on a low setting if your machine has variable settings, then gradually increase once the ingredients have been partially blended, until they are smooth.
- Sprinkle in a few nuts and a spoon or two of fibre-boosting grains, such as rolled oats or quinoa flakes. Add a couple of teaspoons of ground flaxseeds, hulled hemp seeds, sunflower or pumpkin seeds, and complete with a little powdered nutrient-boosting spirulina, wheatgrass or chlorella powder.
- Blend until smooth then pour into a bowl. For a fashionably visual as well as nutritious bowl, decorate with stripes, rings, dots or swirls of fruit purée, cashew cream or yogurt, whole or sliced fruits, tiny cauliflower or broccoli florets, a little shredded kale or lettuce, extra ground or whole seeds, or nuts in patterns on top.
- For the best taste and the highest nutrient content, serve the smoothie bowl the minute it has been prepared.

STEP-BY-STEP SMOOTHIE BOWL

1 Prepare the fruit. In this case, hull some strawberries, chop a lemon and slice a banana.

2 Put the fruit in a blender goblet. For fruit and vegetable mixes with a lower water content, add a little liquid at this stage.

3 Screw on the lid and blend until smooth. Adjust the consistency, if needed, by adding a little extra liquid. Add about 15ml/1 tbsp seeds, chia seeds in this case, and blitz briefly to mix together.

4 Pour the smoothie into a serving bowl. Scrape out all of the smoothie mixture from the blender with a flexible plastic spatula.

5 Decorate and add toppings as you wish. In this case, add small spoonfuls of plain yogurt to the top of the smoothie bowl.

6 Run a skewer or small knife through the yogurt for a marbled effect. If you like, you can arrange sliced strawberries and banana on top and sprinkle with hulled hemp seeds, chia seeds and açaí powder. Serve immediately.

1

2

3

4

5

6

Simply fruity juices

Zingy, colourful and packed with nutrients, fruit juices are a wonderful way to include more fruit in your diet. Whether you like simple combinations of just one or two seasonal fruits, such as peach and strawberry, or watermelon flavoured with star anise, or are up for trying more complex blends made with a number of fruits, there's sure to be something to tantalize your tastebuds in this chapter.

Hum-zinger

This tropical cleanser contains 100 per cent fruit. It will help boost the digestive system and the kidneys, making your eyes sparkle, your hair shine and your skin glow. For the best results, use very ripe fruit, otherwise the juice may be sharp and flavourless. If the fruit is not quite ripe when you buy it, leave it at room temperature for a day or two before juicing. If you like your juices really well chilled, serve with plenty of crushed ice.

Serves 1

½ pineapple, peeled

1 small mango, peeled and pitted

½ small papaya, seeded and peeled

1 Remove any 'eyes' left in the pineapple, then cut all the fruit into chunks. Using a juicer set on low, press through the fruits in the order listed. Alternatively, use a food processor or blender and process the fruit for 2–3 minutes until very smooth.

2 Pour into a glass and serve immediately.

JUICE TIP – Pineapple and mango can produce a very thick juice when blended so, if using this method, you might want to thin it down with a little mineral water before serving.

Citrus sparkle

This vibrantly coloured juice is full of the goodness of natural citrus. These zesty fruits are packed with immune-boosting vitamin C, which can help to ward off winter colds and put a spring in your step, along with valuable folic acid. They are also renowned for their digestive cleansing properties. If you find this blend a little too tart, try adding a natural sweetener, such as honey or agave syrup, and mix the juice well before serving.

Serves 1

1 pink grapefruit

1 orange

30ml/2 tbsp lemon juice

1 Using a sharp knife, cut the grapefruit and orange in half and squeeze out the juice using a citrus juicer.

2 Pour the mixed citrus juice into a tall glass, stir in the lemon juice and serve immediately.

Hum-zinger: Energy 322kcal/1378kJ; Protein 3.7g; Carb 79.2g, of which sugars 78.7g; Fat 1.3g, of which saturates 0.1g; Choll 0mg; Calcium 136mg; Fibre 13.1g; Sodium 21mg
Citrus Sparkle: Energy 92kcal/391kJ; Protein 2.6g; Carb 21.1g, of which sugars 21.1g; Fat 0.3g, of which saturates 0g; Chol 0mg; Calcium 93mg; Fibre 4.1g; Sodium 11mg

Passion fruit and orange

Serves 2

15ml/1 tbsp cardamom pods

15ml/1 tbsp caster/superfine sugar

2 passion fruit

4 large oranges

ice cubes

halved orange slices, to decorate

JUICE TIP – The dark seeds in passion fruit look pretty when suspended in the juice and are edible, but if you don't want them in the drink, press the pulp through a small sieve or strainer with the back of a wooden spoon and just use the juice.

The scent and taste of this juice achieves that perfect balance of aromas and flavours. Sweet, zesty orange juice sits in harmony with aromatic cardamom and intensely fragrant passion fruit to make the most heavenly juice imaginable. What's more, as well as the fabulous flavour and glorious colour, you get a generous shot of vitamin C – what's not to love!

1 Crush the cardamom pods in a mortar with a pestle or place them in a small, metal bowl and pound with the end of a rolling pin until the seeds are exposed.

2 Tip the cardamom pods, with any stray seeds, into a small pan. Add the sugar and stir in 90ml/6 tbsp water. Cover and simmer for 5 minutes.

3 Halve the passion fruit and scoop the pulp into a small jug or pitcher. Squeeze the oranges in a citrus juicer or by hand and tip the juice into the jug.

4 Strain the cardamom syrup through a fine sieve or strainer into the fruit juice and whisk the mixture to distribute the passion fruit and make a light froth.

5 Half-fill two tall glasses with some ice cubes, then pour over the mixed juice. Slip the orange slices into the glasses to serve as edible decoration.

Energy 128kcal/544kJ; Protein 3.2g; Carbohydrate 30g, of which sugars 30g; Fat 0.3g, of which saturates 0g; Cholesterol 0mg; Calcium 123mg; Fibre 4.8g; Sodium 16mg.

Apple shiner

Enjoy radiant skin and an instant energy boost with this cleansing fusion of apple, honeydew melon, red grapes and lemon. This is a good drink to make in the spring, when all of these fruits are widely available. If you cannot get hold of honeydew melon, however, you can use any other type as a substitute in this juice, as long as it's ripe.

Serves 1

450g/1lb or ½ honeydew melon

1 apple

90g/3½oz/⅔ cup seedless red grapes

15ml/1 tbsp lemon juice

1 Using a sharp knife, cut the melon into quarters, scoop out the seeds with a spoon and slice the flesh away from the skin. Quarter the apple and remove the core if you like.

2 Using a juicer, juice the fruit. Alternatively, process the fruit in a food processor or blender for 2–3 minutes until smooth. Pour the juice into a glass, stir in the lemon juice and serve.

JUICE TIP – This drink is refreshingly sharp and tangy, but if you use very sweet apple and melon you might want to add a splash more lemon juice.

Melon pick-me-up

This spicy blend of melon, pear and fresh root ginger will stimulate your circulation and fire you into action. It is a great drink to serve at any time of day, whether you're relaxing with a late breakfast or reviving flagging energy levels at the end of a day's work. Serve the juice really chilled, adding some crushed ice or ice cubes if you like.

Serves 1

2 pears

450g/1lb or ½ cantaloupe melon

2.5cm/1in piece of fresh root ginger, no need to peel

1 Using a sharp knife, quarter the pears. Slice the melon in half and scoop out the seeds with a spoon. Cut the flesh away from the skin, then quarter.

2 Using a juicer, juice all the ingredients, pour into a tall glass and serve immediately.

Apple: Energy 197kcal/842kJ; Protein 3.1g; Carbohydrate 47.8g, of which sugars 47.8g; Fat 0.7g, of which saturates 0g; Cholesterol 0mg; Calcium 79mg; Fibre 3.7g; Sodium 158mg.

Melon: Energy 240kcal/1017kJ; Protein 3.4g; Carbohydrate 58g, of which sugars 58g; Fat 0.8g, of which saturates 0g; Cholesterol 0mg; Calcium 98mg; Fibre 8.6g; Sodium 164mg.

Pink and perky

This deliciously refreshing, rose-tinged blend of grapefruit and pear juice will keep you bright-eyed and bushy-tailed. It's perfect for a quick breakfast drink or as a pick-me-up later in the day when energy levels are flagging.

1 Take a thin slice from one grapefruit half and cut a few thin slices of pear. Quarter the remaining pear lengthways and press through a juicer.

2 Squeeze all the juice from the grapefruit halves with a citrus juicer. Mix the fruit juices together and serve over ice. Decorate with the grapefruit and pear slices.

Serves 2

1 pink and 1 white grapefruit, halved

2 ripe pears

ice cubes

JUICE TIP – If the grapefruit is particularly tart, serve the juice with a little bowl of brown sugar on the side so that you can sweeten it to taste.

Energy 108kcal/455kJ; Protein 1.8g; Carbohydrate 25.9g, of which sugars 25.9g; Fat 0.3g, of which saturates 0g; Cholesterol 0mg; Calcium 54mg; Fibre 5.4g; Sodium 10mg.

Sweet, sharp shock

Serves 1

150g/5oz/1 cup seedless red grapes

1 red-skinned eating apple, no need to peel or core

1 small cooking apple

crushed ice

JUICE TIP – The simplest flavour combinations are often the most delicious. Sugary grapes together with mouth-puckeringly tart apples is one of those perfect pairings that simply cannot be beaten.

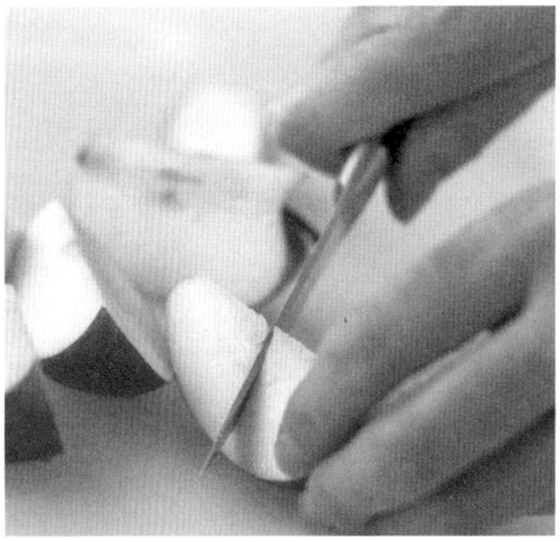

The taste-tingling combination of sweet red grape and tart apple is quite delicious. Grapes are full of natural sugars and, mixed with apple juice, they'll create a juice that's full of pep and zing. Grapes are also renowned for their cleansing properties, making this an ideal addition to any detox regime. For a longer, more refreshing drink, top up with sparkling mineral water.

1 Slice some grapes and apple slivers for decoration. Chop the remaining apples. Press through a juicer with the grapes.

2 Pour the juice over crushed ice, decorate with the sliced fruit and serve immediately.

Energy 178kcal/763kJ; Protein 1.4g; Carbohydrate 45.4g, of which sugars 45.4g; Fat 0.4g, of which saturates 0g; Cholesterol 0mg; Calcium 30mg; Fibre 5g; Sodium 8mg.

Watermelon and star anise fizz

Serves 2

15g/½oz star anise

15ml/1 tbsp caster/superfine sugar

500g/1¼lb wedge of watermelon

sparkling mineral water

JUICE TIP – Sweet, scented, frothy pink bubbles make this a heavenly non-alcoholic cocktail to serve at parties. Or enjoy it as a cooling thirst-quencher on a long, hot summer afternoon.

The delicate taste of watermelon becomes surprisingly intense when juiced, so to balance it, additional flavours need to be equally pronounced. A light syrup infused with scented star anise is the perfect choice. For maximum impact, make sure the star anise is really fresh as its liquorice-like flavour and aroma tend to fade with age.

1 Roughly crush the star anise in a mortar using a pestle, or place it in a small metal bowl and pound with the end of a rolling pin.

2 Tip the crushed spice into a small pan and add the sugar and 90ml/6 tbsp water. Bring to the boil, stirring, then let it bubble for about 2 minutes. Remove the pan from the heat and leave to steep for 10 minutes.

3 Cut off and discard the rind from the watermelon and, using a small, sharp knife, cut the flesh into chunks of roughly the same size, removing all of the hard black seeds.

4 Press the melon chunks through a juicer. Strain the anise syrup through a fine sieve or strainer and pour it into the melon juice. Stir well to mix the flavours together thoroughly.

5 Fill your glasses two-thirds full with the juice, then top up with sparkling water and serve immediately.

Energy 107kcal/459kJ; Protein 1.3g; Carbohydrate 25.6g, of which sugars 25.6g; Fat 0.8g, of which saturates 0.3g; Cholesterol 0mg; Calcium 22mg; Fibre 0.3g; Sodium 6mg.

Fragrant fruits

This blend of sweet and subtle fruits packs a surprising punch. It combines a splash of lemon and a hint of fresh root ginger to add zest and bite without overpowering the delicate, fragrant flavours of lychee, cantaloupe and pear. Other types of melon can be used in place of the cantaloupe, but you will lose the pretty colour that is part of this juice's appeal.

Serves 2

10 lychees

1 large pear

300g/11oz wedge of cantaloupe melon, rind removed

2cm/¾in piece of fresh root ginger, no need to peel, roughly chopped

squeeze of lemon juice

crushed ice

mint sprigs, to decorate

1 Peel and pit the lychees and, using a sharp knife, cut both the pear and the melon into large chunks.

2 Press the ginger through a juicer, followed by the lychees, pear and finally the melon. Sharpen the flavour with a little of the lemon juice to taste.

3 Place the crushed ice and one or two mint sprigs in two glasses and pour over the juice. Place some more mint sprigs on top to decorate, then serve the juice immediately – before the ice melts.

JUICE TIP – Sweet, scented lychee and perfectly ripe cantaloupe melon shine through in this gloriously fragrant, delicately coloured blend of fresh fruits. To say that this drink is simply delicious is understating its qualities – not only is it subtle and refreshing, but it is also extremely good for you. If you want to be a little wicked, though, add a dash of vodka – it will add an extra-special kick.

Energy 110kcal/466kJ; Protein 1.7g; Carbohydrate 26.7g, of which sugars 26.7g; Fat 0.3g, of which saturates 0g; Cholesterol 0mg; Calcium 33mg; Fibre 2.8g; Sodium 50mg.

Minty melon cooler

Serves 3–4

1 Galia or cantaloupe melon
several large mint sprigs
juice of 2 large limes
ice cubes
extra mint sprigs and lime slices, to decorate

JUICE TIP – To tell whether a melon is ripe or not, it is best to use your nose. It should smell fragrant around the area where the stem was, at the top of the melon, but not too strong or it could be overripe. When buying, choose one that feels relatively heavy.

The wonderfully juicy flesh of ripe melon seems somehow more fragrant when juiced. A dash of lime cuts through the sweetness perfectly and zips up the flavour, while refreshing, peppery mint makes a classic, cool companion to both. This mellow soother is equally calming and stimulating – what a combination.

1 Halve and seed the melon and cut into wedges. Cut one wedge into long, thin slices and reserve for decoration.

2 Cut the skin from the remaining melon wedges and press half the melon through a juicer.

3 Strip the mint leaves from the sprigs, press them through the juicer, then juice the remaining melon.

4 Stir in the lime juice and then pour the juice over ice cubes in three or four glasses. Decorate with mint sprigs and lime slices. Add a slice of melon to each glass and serve.

Energy 45kcal/191kJ; Protein 1g; Carbohydrate 10.5g, of which sugars 10.5g; Fat 0.2g, of which saturates 0g; Cholesterol; 0mg; Calcium 25mg; Fibre 0.8g; Sodium 58mg.

Lavender and order

Serves 4–6

10–12 lavender flowers, plus extra stems, for stirrers

45ml/3 tbsp caster/superfine sugar

8 large oranges

ice cubes

JUICE TIP – Be careful about where you pick your lavender – it can collect dust and pollution if it is near a road. It is probably worth washing it, too, to ensure it is clean before you use it in your drink.

This fragrant, lavender-scented juice is guaranteed to perk up a jaded palate in no time at all. Its heavenly aroma and distinct yet subtle taste is quite divine. Make plenty and keep it in the fridge, adding a few extra lavender sprigs to intensify the flavour, if you like.

1 Pull the lavender flowers from their stalks and put them in a bowl with the sugar plus 120ml/4fl oz boiling water. Stir until the sugar has dissolved, then leave for 10 minutes.

2 Squeeze the oranges using a citrus juicer and pour the juice into a jug. Strain the lavender syrup into the juice. Chill.

3 Put a few ice cubes and a couple of lavender stirrers in some glasses, top up with the juice and serve.

Energy 91kcal/389kJ; Protein 1.9g; Carbohydrate 22g, of which sugars 22g; Fat 0.2g, of which saturates 0g; Cholesterol 0mg; Calcium 82mg; Fibre 2.8g; Sodium 9mg.

Pomegranate plus

The exotic and distinctive flavour of pomegranate is quite delicious. A reddish skin is usually a sign that the seeds inside will be vibrant and sweet. Pomegranate juice makes a fabulous base for this treat of a juice, which is mildly spiced with a hint of fresh ginger.

1 Halve the pomegranates. Working over a bowl to catch the juices, pull away the skin to remove the seeds.

2 Quarter the figs and roughly chop the ginger. Press the figs and ginger through a juicer. Press the pomegranate seeds through, too, reserving a few for decoration. Stir in the lime juice.

3 Pour over ice cubes and lime wedges in glasses, then serve.

Serves 2

2 pomegranates
4 fresh figs
15g/½oz fresh root ginger, no need to peel
10ml/2 tsp lime juice
ice cubes
lime wedges

JUICE TIP – Pomegranates are refreshing in hot weather, especially when combined with figs, ginger and lime juice. Serve this ice-cold to quench a summer thirst.

Energy 224kcal/951kJ; Protein 3.4g; Carbohydrate 52.3g, of which sugars 52.3g; Fat 1.6g, of which saturates 0g; Cholesterol 0mg; Calcium 233mg; Fibre 6.9g; Sodium 58mg.

Tropical calm

This deliciously scented juice is packed with the cancer-fighting antioxidant betacarotene and can aid liver and kidney function to cleanse and purify the system. This is a quick and easy drink to make at any time, whether you're rushing out in the morning or relaxing later in the day. If you're really thirsty, it's a good blend to top up with plenty of chilled sparkling water.

Serves 1

1 papaya

450g/1lb or ½ cantaloupe melon

90g/3½oz/⅔ cup seedless white grapes

1 Using a sharp knife, halve and skin the papaya, remove the seeds and then cut the flesh into rough slices. Halve the melon, scoop out the seeds and cut into quarters. Slice the flesh away from the skin and cut into chunks.

2 Juice the papaya, melon and grapes using a juicer, or blend in a food processor or blender for a thicker juice. Serve immediately.

JUICE TIP - Some varieties of papaya stay green when ripe, but most turn yellowy-orange and soften slightly. They bruise easily so don't buy any that have been knocked about. The seeds are not tasty, so discard them.

Strawberry soother

Juices don't come much purer than this one. Made with fresh, ripe strawberries and a succulent peach or nectarine, depending on your preference, nothing else at all is added to this comforting blend. Rich in vitamin C, calcium and healing phytochemicals, strawberries are a good addition to any detox diet, while peaches and nectarines are great for healthier skin.

Serves 1

1 peach or nectarine

225g/8oz/2 cups strawberries

1 Using a sharp knife, quarter the peach or nectarine and pull out the pit. Cut the flesh into rough slices or chunks ready for juicing. Hull the strawberries.

2 Juice the fruit, using a juicer, or blend in a food processor or blender for a thicker juice. Serve immediately.

Tropical: Energy 294kcal/1251kJ; Protein 4.4g; Carbohydrate 71.5g, of which sugars 71.5g; Fat 0.9g, of which saturates 0g; Cholesterol 0mg; Calcium 156mg; Fibre 11g; Sodium 146mg.

Strawberry: Energy 84kcal/354kJ; Protein 2.5g; Carbohydrate 18.8g, of which sugars 18.8g; Fat 0.3g, of which saturates 0g; Cholesterol 0mg; Calcium 41mg; Fibre 3.5g; Sodium 14mg.

Peachy pleasure

Serves 2

4 kumquats
6 ripe apricots, pitted
2 peaches, pitted
clear honey, to taste
ice cubes

JUICE TIP – This drink is ideal for informal parties as well as a quick breakfast. If you are having friends round for dinner or drinks, make some cocktail-style stirrers. Simply halve some apricots, thread them on to long wooden skewers and place a skewer in each glass.

When juiced together, apricots, peaches and kumquats produce amazingly vibrant orange-coloured juice with a flavour that has just as big a kick – and it is utterly delicious. The natural sugar content of apricots and peaches can vary so you will need to add some honey to get the taste just right.

1 Roughly chop the kumquats and cut the apricots and peaches into large chunks. (There is no need to peel the fruit.)

2 Press the kumquat pieces through a juicer, followed by the apricot and peach chunks, alternating the fruit as you go to ensure they mix well.

3 Fill large glasses with ice cubes and pour the fruit juice over the ice. Stir in a little honey to the juice and taste. Add a little more honey if the juice is not sweet enough. (Be careful not to add too much honey, however, or it will overpower the other flavours and spoil the drink.) Serve immediately.

The tropicana

Serves 2–3

1 large papaya
1 persimmon
1 large guava
juice of 2 oranges
2 passion fruit, halved

Even in winter this drink can brighten your day with its lively colour and fruity flavour. Any blend of tropical fruits can be used as long as they are ripe. Persimmon and guavas can be quite bitter if juiced when underripe so, if necessary, leave the fruits in the fruit bowl to ripen for a few days before using.

1 Halve the papaya, then scoop out and discard the black seeds. Cut the papaya, persimmon and guava flesh into large chunks of roughly the same size. (There's no need to peel them.)

2 Press the papaya through a juicer, followed by the persimmon and the guava. Pour the juice into a jug or pitcher, then add the orange juice and scoop in the passion fruit pulp. Whisk and chill until ready to serve.

Peachy: Energy 78kcal/335kJ; Protein 2.3g; Carbohydrate 18g, of which sugars 18g; Fat 0.3g, of which saturates 0g; Cholesterol 0mg; Calcium 31mg; Fibre 3.8g; Sodium 4mg.
Tropicana: Energy 85kcal/361kJ; Protein 1.8g; Carbohydrate 19.3g, of which sugars 19.2g; Fat 0.6g, of which saturates 0g; Cholesterol 0mg; Calcium 45mg; Fibre 6g; Sodium 17mg.

Cherry berry trio

Strawberries and grapes have long been reputed to cleanse and purify the system, while cherries and strawberries are rich in vitamin C. This juice needs no sweetening.

Serves 2

200g/7oz/1¾ cups strawberries

250g/9oz/1¾ cups seedless red grapes

150g/5oz/1¼ cups red cherries, pitted

ice cubes

1 Halve two or three strawberries and grapes and set aside with a few cherries for decoration. Cut up any large strawberries, then press through a juicer with the remaining grapes and cherries.

2 Pour into two glasses, top with the halved fruits, cherries and ice cubes, and serve. To make a decoration, skewer a halved strawberry or grape on a cocktail stick and hang a cherry by its stem.

Energy 138kcal/587kJ; Protein 2g; Carbohydrate 33.9g, of which sugars 33.9g; Fat 0.3g, of which saturates 0g; Cholesterol 0mg; Calcium 42mg; Fibre 2.7g; Sodium 10mg.

Blue lagoon

Serves 1

90g/3½oz/scant 1 cup blackcurrants or blackberries

150g/5oz/1 cup seedless red grapes

130g/4½oz/generous 1 cup blueberries

ice cubes

Blueberries are an excellent source of betacarotene and vitamin C, and are also rich in flavonoids, which help to cleanse the system. Mixed with other dark red fruits, such as blackberries and grapes, they make a highly nutritious blend.

1 Pull the blackcurrants, if using, and grapes from their stalks.

2 Press the fruits through a juicer, saving a few for decoration. Place the ice in a medium glass and pour over the juice. Decorate with the remaining fruit and serve.

Energy 189kcal/805kJ; Protein 2.7g; Carbohydrate 47.2g, of which sugars 42g; Fat 0.2g, of which saturates 0g; Cholesterol 0mg; Calcium 74mg; Fibre 6.9g; Sodium 6mg.

Gooseberry refresher

Combine a sharp, tangy fruit like gooseberries with the sweetness of apples, greengages and kiwi fruit for a perfect blend of flavours – not too sweet, not too sharp. Even better, this drink is loaded up with vital vitamins and minerals, meaning you can enjoy this delicious, healthy tonic guilt-free. You can use thawed frozen gooseberries when they are not in season.

1 Peel the kiwi fruit, then halve and pit the greengages. Core and roughly chop the apple.

2 Press the kiwi fruit, greengages, apple and gooseberries through a juicer and pour over ice cubes into a glass. Add one or two gooseberries to decorate.

Serves 1

1 kiwi fruit

2 greengages

1 eating apple

90g/3½oz/scant 1 cup gooseberries, plus extra to decorate

ice cubes

JUICE TIP - Pink-tinged dessert gooseberries tend to be sweeter than the green ones, but both taste good in this refreshing drink so use whatever you can get your hands on.

Energy 92kcal/391kJ; Protein 2.2g; Carbohydrate 20.3g, of which sugars 20.1g; Fat 0.8g, of which saturates 0g; Cholesterol 0mg; Calcium 51mg; Fibre 5.3g; Sodium 7mg.

Kiwi and ginger spritzer

Serves 1

2 kiwi fruit

1 piece of preserved stem ginger, plus 15ml/1 tbsp syrup from the ginger jar

sparkling mineral water

JUICE TIP – Kiwis are a subtropical fruit, not a tropical one, so it is best to store them in the fridge before using. If you want them to ripen quickly, store in a closed plastic bag with an apple, pear or banana.

The delicate, refreshingly tangy flavour of kiwi fruit becomes sweeter and more intense when the flesh is juiced. Choose plump, unwrinkled fruits that give a little when gently pressed as under-ripe fruits will produce a slightly bitter taste. A single kiwi fruit contains more than one day's vitamin C requirement, so this juice will boost the system.

1 Roughly chop the kiwi fruit and the ginger. (For a better colour you can peel the kiwi fruit first, but this is not essential.)

2 Press the kiwi fruit and ginger through a juicer and pour the juice into a jug or pitcher. Stir in the ginger syrup.

3 Pour the juice into a tall glass, then top up with sparkling mineral water and serve immediately.

Energy 104kcal/439kJ; Protein 1.4g; Carbohydrate 24.6g, of which sugars 24.2g; Fat 0.6g, of which saturates 0g; Cholesterol 0mg; Calcium 32mg; Fibre 2.3g; Sodium 45mg.

Spiced pomegranate pear fizz

Serves 2

2 Asian pears

1.5ml/¼ tsp ground allspice

1 pomegranate

5–10ml/1–2 tsp clear honey

ice cubes

tonic water

pear wedges and pomegranate seeds, to decorate

NUTRIENT NOTE – Ideal for slimmers, pears are virtually fat-free and contain absolutely no cholesterol or sodium. They also provide significant amounts of vitamin C and potassium.

Sweet but with a milder flavour than traditional pears, Asian pears make a good partner for the fresh tang of pomegranates. Juice the fruits in advance if you have the time, so the spice can mellow into the fruits, all ready for topping up with fizzy tonic water.

1 Using a small, sharp knife, chop the pears into large chunks. Mix the allspice in a jug or pitcher with 15ml/1 tbsp boiling water.

2 Halve the pomegranate. Working over the large bowl to catch the juices, peel away the skin and layers of pith to leave the clusters of seeds.

3 Press the pears and pomegranate seeds through a juicer. Mix in the jug with the allspice. Stir in honey to sweeten, then chill.

4 Pour the juice into two glasses until two-thirds full. Serve with ice cubes, pear wedges and pomegranate seeds to decorate. Top up with tonic water.

Elderflower, plum and ginger

Serves 2–3

15g/½oz fresh root ginger, no need to peel

500g/1lb 2oz ripe plums

125ml/4½fl oz/generous ½ cup sweet elderflower cordial

ice cubes

sparkling water or tonic water

mint sprigs and plum slices, to decorate

Captured in cordials and juices, the aromatic flavour of elderflowers can be enjoyed all year round. Here, it is used with fresh root ginger to give an exotic boost to sweet, juicy plums. Serve this as it is over plenty of crushed ice or top up with sparkling water, if you prefer a more diluted drink.

1 Roughly chop the ginger without peeling it. Halve and pit the plums. Press half the plums through a juicer, then the ginger, then the remaining plums. Mix the juice with the elderflower cordial in a jug or pitcher.

2 Pour the juice into two or three glasses until two-thirds full. Top up with sparkling mineral water or tonic water, decorate with the mint sprigs and plum slices, and serve immediately.

Pomegranate: Energy 92kcal/391kJ; Protein 0.6g; Carbohydrate 23.3g, of which sugars 23.3g; Fat 0.2g, of which saturates 0g; Cholesterol 0mg; Calcium 19mg; Fibre 4.1g; Sodium 6mg.
Elderflower: Energy 105kcal/450kJ; Protein 1g; Carbohydrate 26.6g, of which sugars 26.6g; Fat 0.2g, of which saturates 0g; Cholesterol 0mg; Calcium 25mg; Fibre 2.7g; Sodium 7mg.

Fruit and vegetable juices

When your energy levels are flagging, these drinks are guaranteed to perk you up. Made using pure vegetables and fruit with no additives, they serve a variety of purposes, from detoxing and cleansing the body to healing and energizing the mind. Ready in minutes, blends including carrot, fennel, tomato and spinach are a sure-fire way to drink yourself healthy.

Bright eyes

Serves 2

200g/7oz or 1 large carrot

6 clementines, plus extra wedges to decorate, if liked

ice cubes

JUICE TIP - Take the tingle factor up a notch by adding some spice. Peel and slice some fresh root ginger and press it through the juicer with the clementines and carrots.

Thin-skinned citrus fruits like clementines can be put through the juicer without peeling, adding a zesty kick to the final mix – and saving time when you're in a hurry. This vibrant, intensely flavoured carrot and clementine combination is packed with vitamin A, which is essential for healthy vision, and vitamin C to give an extra boost to the whole system.

1 Scrub the carrots and, using a sharp knife, chop them into large chunks. Quarter the clementines, discarding any pips.

2 Press the clementine quarters through a juicer, then repeat the procedure with the carrot chunks. Pour the juice over ice cubes in two glasses and decorate each glass with a wedge of clementine, if you like.

Energy 71kcal/299kJ; Protein 1.6g; Carbohydrate 16.4g, of which sugars 16g; Fat 0.4g, of which saturates 0.1g; Cholesterol 0mg; Calcium 56mg; Fibre 3.3g; Sodium 24mg.

Veggie boost

This simple blend has pure, clean flavours and a chilli kick that is guaranteed to revitalize flagging energy levels. Tomatoes and carrots are rich in the valuable antioxidant betacarotene, which is reputed to fight cancer, and they contain a good supply of vitamins A, C and E.

1 Quarter the tomatoes and roughly chop the chilli. (If you prefer a milder juice, remove the seeds and white pith from the chilli before chopping.) Scrub the carrots and chop them roughly.

2 Press the carrots through a juicer, followed by the tomatoes and chilli. Add the orange juice and stir well to mix. Fill two glasses with crushed ice, pour the juice over and serve.

Serves 2

3 tomatoes
1 fresh red or green chilli
250g/9oz or 2 small carrots
juice of 1 orange
crushed ice

JUICE TIP - Non-organic carrots often contain a lot of chemicals in their skins, so scrub them well or peel them.

Energy 84kcal/351kJ; Protein 2.7g; Carbohydrate 16.9g, of which sugars 16.3g; Fat 1g, of which saturates 0.3g; Cholesterol 0mg; Calcium 52mg; Fibre 4.6g; Sodium 49mg.

Tarragon, orange and tomato

Lovers of tomato juice are sure to get hooked on this flavour-packed, vitalizing blend. Fresh orange makes it irresistibly moreish and adds extra vitamin C, while tarragon adds a lovely aromatic note. Add a dash of Tabasco or chilli sauce instead of the ground black pepper if you simply cannot resist the classic combination of chilli and tomato.

Serves 2–4

4 large tarragon sprigs, plus extra to decorate (optional)

500g/1lb 2oz tomatoes

2 large oranges

15ml/1 tbsp sun-dried tomato paste

ice cubes

ground black pepper, to taste

1 Pull the tarragon leaves from their stalks. Roughly chop the tomatoes if they are large. Press them through a juicer, alternating with the tarragon leaves.

2 Squeeze the juice from the oranges by hand or using a citrus juicer. Stir into the tomato and tarragon juice. Add the sun-dried tomato paste and stir well to mix all the ingredients together.

3 Place ice cubes into some glasses and pour over the juice. Serve immediately with pretty stirrers (if you have them), a sprinkling of black pepper to taste, and tarragon sprigs to decorate, if you like.

Energy 93kcal/397kJ; Protein 3.5g; Carbohydrate 19g, of which sugars 19g; Fat 0.9g, of which saturates 0.3g; Cholesterol 0mg; Calcium 77mg; Fibre 4.8g; Sodium 47mg.

Tomato and basil blush

Some herbs just don't juice well, losing their aromatic flavour and turning muddy and dull. Basil, however, is an excellent juicer, keeping its distinctive fresh fragrance. It makes the perfect partner for mild, refreshing cucumber and the ripest, juiciest tomatoes you can find.

1 Quarter the cucumber lengthways – do not remove the seeds. Press it through a juicer with the basil, then press through the tomatoes and stir to blend.

2 Pour the blended tomato, basil and cucumber juice over cubes of ice in one or two glasses and serve decorated with a few fresh sprigs of basil.

Serves 1–2

½ cucumber, peeled

a handful of fresh basil, plus extra to decorate

350g/12oz tomatoes

ice cubes

JUICE TIP – You don't have to peel the cucumber, but the juice will have a fresher, lighter colour without peel.

Energy 40kcal/168kJ; Protein 1.9g; Carbohydrate 7g, of which sugars 6.8g; Fat 0.7g, of which saturates 0.2g; Cholesterol 0mg; Calcium 31mg; Fibre 2.4g; Sodium 19mg.

Ruby roots

Serves 1

200g/7oz or 2 medium beetroot/ beets, scrubbed

1cm/½in piece of fresh root ginger, no need to peel

1 large orange

ice cubes

Beetroot has the highest sugar content of any vegetable and, not surprisingly, makes one of the sweetest juices, with a vibrant red colour and a rich yet refreshing taste. Despite its firm texture, beetroot can be juiced raw and its intense flavour combines wonderfully with tangy citrus fruits and fresh root ginger. Enjoy this juice as a natural cleanser.

1 Trim the beetroot and cut into quarters. Press half through a juicer, followed by the ginger and remaining beetroot.

2 Squeeze the juice from the orange with a citrus juicer and mix it with the beetroot juice. Pour the blended juice over ice cubes in a glass or clear glass cup. Serve immediately.

Energy 90kcal/385kJ; Protein 3.6g; Carbohydrate 19.6g, of which sugars 18.4g; Fat 0.3g, of which saturates 0g; Cholesterol 0mg; Calcium 45mg; Fibre 3.8g; Sodium 137mg.

Citrus beet blast

During intense exercise you not only lose water through sweat but also minerals. Rehydration is key but it is also important to boost mineral and energy levels too, to aid recovery time. Packed with concentrated goodness, this is one super-charged juice.

Serves 1–2

25g/1oz/1 cup baby spinach leaves

3 cavolo nero or black kale leaves

1 green apple, no need to peel or core

150g/5oz or 1 carrot, scrubbed

75g/3oz or 1 small beetroot/beet, scrubbed and trimmed

½ large orange, peel and pith cut away

175ml/6fl oz/¾ cup water

5ml/1 tsp honey, maple syrup or a sweetener of your choice

1 Pack the spinach into the feeder chute of the juicer then gradually press all the remaining fruit and vegetables through.

2 Stir the water into the juice, pour into one or two glasses and sweeten to taste.

JUICE TIP – A small handful of shredded green kale can be used in place of the cavolo nero if preferred.

NUTRIENT NOTE – Naturally sweet beetroot contains the equivalent of 5ml/1 tsp of sugar per 100g/3¾oz, so this juice is a great way to boost energy levels, plus it contains folates, vitamin C, iron and potassium, which helps to regulate blood pressure and nerve function. The high levels of nitrates have been shown to benefit cyclists and marathon runners before a race, to sustain them and keep them energized over long distances. Just make sure to take it to events in a well-sealed container!

Energy 112kcal/474kJ; Protein 4.7g; Carbohydrate 21.9g, of which sugars 21.8g; Fat 1.2g, of which saturates 0.1g; Cholesterol 0mg; Calcium 259mg; Fibre 0.9g; Sodium 230mg.

Turbo-charged beet

Refuel your body with this tangy, refreshing, homemade isotonic sports drink. Betacyanin is the pigment that gives beetroot its intense colour; if consumed regularly it is thought it may help reduce the oxidation of LDL cholesterol and so help protect artery walls and reduce the risk of heart disease and stroke.

1 Gradually press all the vegetables then fruit through the juicer.

2 Stir in the coconut water then pour into a tall glass half-filled with ice cubes, and serve.

Serves 1

25g/1oz or ⅓ small beetroot/beet, scrubbed and trimmed

50g/2oz/2 cups shredded kale

¼ medium pineapple, peeled, but core left in or 200g/7oz/1 cup prepared pineapple, cut into chunks

1 green apple, no need to peel or core

125ml/4fl oz/½ cup coconut water from a carton

ice cubes, to serve

Energy 118kcal/506kJ; Protein 3g; Carbohydrate 25.7g, of which sugars 25.5g; Fat 1.2g, of which saturates 0.1g; Cholesterol 0mg; Calcium 100mg; Fibre 1.3g; Sodium 43mg.

Antioxidant superfusion

The brighter the colour of the fruit and vegetable, the more antioxidants and phytochemicals there will be. These help to reduce the activity of free radicals in the body, which can damage DNA and body tissues, and can protect against disease. Think of this juice rather like drinking in a rainbow.

Serves 1–2

25g/1oz/1 cup shredded kale

50g/2oz/½ cup broccoli florets and sliced stem

2 green apples, no need to peel or core

150g/5oz or 1 carrot, scrubbed

50g/2oz or 1 small chunk of red cabbage

ice cubes, to serve (optional)

1 Gradually press all the vegetables and fruit through the juicer then pour into one or two glasses over ice cubes, if liked.

JUICE TIP – This juice is super-concentrated so you might like to top it up with a little extra mineral water.

Energy 177kcal/758kJ; Protein 4.8g; Carbohydrate 38.1g, of which sugars 37.8g; Fat 1.8g, of which saturates 0.5g; Cholesterol 0mg; Calcium 142mg; Fibre 8.6g; Sodium 158mg.

Red hot chilli pepper

Serves 2–3

2 red bell peppers

1 fresh red chilli, seeded

150g/5oz or 1 small courgette/zucchini

75g/3oz radishes

1 orange

ice cubes

JUICE TIP – When working with chillies, always wash your hands thoroughly after chopping them. Avoid touching your eyes or any other delicate area because it really will sting.

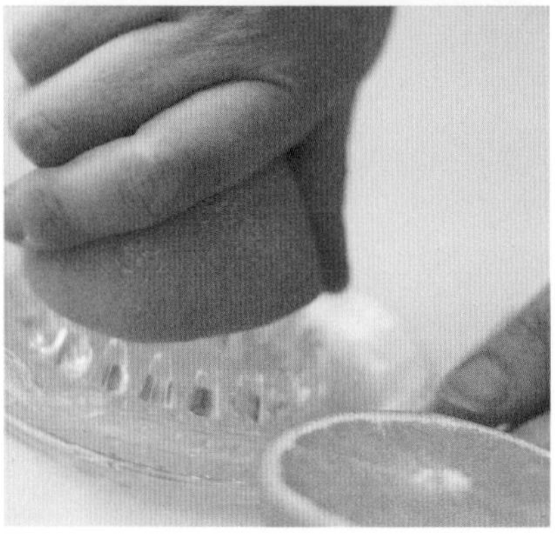

Sweet red peppers make a colourful, light juice that's best mixed with other ingredients for a full flavour impact. Courgettes add a subtle, almost unnoticeable body to the drink, while chilli and radishes bring a wonderful kick of peppery heat. Freshly squeezed orange juice gives a delicious underlying zest to this quaffable beverage.

1 Halve the peppers, remove the cores and seeds, quarter the pieces and press them through a juicer with the chilli. Cut the courgettes into chunks, halve the radishes and press them through the juicer.

2 Squeeze the orange juice and stir it into the vegetable juice. Fill two or three glasses with ice, pour over the juice and serve.

Energy 64kcal/269kJ; Protein 2.7g; Carbohydrate 12.2g, of which sugars 11.8g; Fat 0.8g, of which saturates 0.2g; Cholesterol 0mg; Calcium 45mg; Fibre 3.2g; Sodium 10mg.

Clean sweep

This juice is so packed with goodness, you can almost feel it cleansing and detoxing your body. As well as valuable vitamins, the carrots and grapes provide plenty of natural sweetness, which blends perfectly with the mild pepperiness of the celery and fresh scent of parsley. Drink this juice on a regular basis to give your system a thorough clean-out.

1 Using a sharp knife, roughly chop the celery and carrots. Press half of the celery, carrots and grapes through a juicer, then add the parsley sprigs. Add the remaining celery, carrots and grapes in the same way and juice until thoroughly combined.

2 Pour the juice into one or two glasses and serve with celery or carrot stick stirrers.

Serves 1–2

1 celery stick

300g/11oz or 2 carrots, scrubbed

150g/5oz/1 cup seedless green grapes

several large sprigs of parsley

celery or carrot sticks, for stirrers

JUICE TIP – When juicing herbs, do not remove their individual stalks because it is these that contain much of the goodness and flavour – and they go through the juicing machine really easily.

NUTRIENT NOTE – Parsley contains calcium, vitamins and iron and also works as a natural cleanser and breath freshener.

Energy 99kcal/417kJ; Protein 1.3g; Carbohydrate 23.6g, of which sugars 22.8g; Fat 0.6g, of which saturates 0.2g; Cholesterol 0mg; Calcium 54mg; Fibre 1.3g; Sodium 48mg.

Kale and red cabbage rainbow

Serves 1

25g/1oz/1 cup shredded or whole kale leaves

175g/6oz or 1 courgette/ zucchini

150g/5oz or 1 carrot, scrubbed

75g/3oz or 1 small parsnip, scrubbed

75g/3oz/scant 1 cup roughly chopped red cabbage

1 celery stick

1 green apple, no need to peel or core

2.5ml/½ tsp wheatgrass powder

A rainbow of colour, don't stir this juice until you are just about to serve it – ideally straight after making it. Packed with pure concentrated goodness, it is full of vitamins, minerals, phytochemicals and antioxidants to help fight infection, give strength to muscles, skin, bone and other tissues, and boost production of white blood cells.

1 Press the kale into the feeder chute of the juicer, then gradually press through all the remaining ingredients apart from the wheatgrass powder.

2 Whisk in the wheatgrass powder, pour the juice into a tall glass and serve immediately.

Energy 190kcal/796kJ; Protein 7.5g; Carbohydrate 35.7g, of which sugars 29.3g; Fat 2.7g, of which saturates 0.5g; Cholesterol 0mg; Calcium 204mg; Fibre 1.7g; Sodium 84mg.

Fennel fusion

This hefty combination of raw vegetables and apples makes a surprisingly tasty juice – fresh fennel has a distinctive aniseed flavour that blends well with both fruit and vegetables. Cabbage has natural antibacterial properties, while apples and fennel can help to cleanse the system. As an equally refreshing alternative, use two or three sticks of celery instead of the fennel.

1 Roughly slice the fennel and cut the apples into quarters. Press the vegetables and fruit through a juicer.

2 Add the lemon juice to the juice and stir to combine. Pour into a glass and serve immediately.

Serves 1

½ fennel bulb

2 apples, no need to peel or core

75g/3oz/scant 1 cup roughly chopped red cabbage

15ml/1 tbsp lemon juice

JUICE TIP – Buy really firm, fresh-looking fennel. If it is old, its outer leaves quickly discolour and it becomes fibrous.

Apple and leaf lift-off

This blend of apple, grapes, fresh leaves and lime juice is the perfect rejuvenator and is great for treating skin, liver and kidney disorders. Apples play a part in so many delicious and healthy blends that it's worth buying a large bag that will keep well in the fridge for several days. Most varieties can be juiced successfully so simply choose your favourite kind, or whatever is available.

1 Using a sharp knife, quarter the apple, removing the core if you like. Press half of the apple quarters and the grapes through a juicer, followed by the coriander and the watercress or rocket, then the remaining apple quarters.

2 Add the lime juice to the fruit and herb mixture and stir well. Pour the mixture into a tall glass and serve immediately.

Serves 1

1 apple

150g/5oz/1 cup seedless white grapes

small handful of fresh coriander/cilantro, stalks included

25g/1oz/1 cup watercress or rocket/arugula leaves

15ml/1 tbsp lime juice

Fennel: Energy 183kcal/779kJ; Protein 5.5g; Carbs 40.3g, of which sugars 39.9g; Fat 1.1g, of which saturates 0g; Cholesterol 0mg; Calcium 158mg; Fibre 2.8g; Sodium 42mg
Apple: Energy 135kcal/581kJ; Protein 3.8g; Carbs 29.5g, of which sugars 29.5g; Fat 1.2g, of which saturates 0.3g; Cholesterol 0mg; Calcium 192mg; Fibre 3.6g; Sodium 53mg.

Fennel and parsnip pep

Serves 4–5

115g/4oz fennel

200g/7oz or 2 parsnips, scrubbed

1 apple

1 pear

a small handful of flat leaf parsley

ice cubes

Although parsnips yield a relatively small amount of juice, the juicer produces an amazingly thick, sweet and creamy drink, adding body to any raw fruit and vegetable blend. Refreshing fennel, apple and pear are the perfect foils for the intense sweetness of parsnip and together create this tantalizing power-pack of a fresh juice.

1 Cut the fennel and parsnips into similar-sized large chunks. Quarter the apple and pear, removing the core, if you like, then cut the quartered pieces in half.

2 Press half the fruit and vegetables through a juicer, then follow with the parsley and the remaining fruit and vegetables. Place ice cubes in shot glasses and pour the juice over. Serve immediately.

Energy 113kcal/477kJ; Protein 2.7g; Carbohydrate 24g, of which sugars 17.2g; Fat 1.3g, of which saturates 0.2g; Cholesterol 0mg; Calcium 65mg; Fibre 2.2g; Sodium 19mg.

Ginger and carrot juice

Fresh root ginger is one of the best natural cures for indigestion and it helps to settle upset stomachs or motion sickness. In this unusual fruity blend, it is simply mixed with fresh, juicy pineapple and sweet-tasting carrot, for a quick and easy remedy that can be juiced up in minutes – it tastes delicious too.

1 Cut away the skin from the pineapple, then halve and remove the core. Roughly slice the pineapple flesh. Peel and roughly chop the ginger, then chop the carrot.

2 Press the carrot, ginger and pineapple through a juicer and pour into a glass. Add ice cubes and serve immediately.

Serves 1

½ small pineapple
25g/1oz fresh root ginger, no need to peel
150g/5oz or 1 carrot, scrubbed
ice cubes

JUICE TIP – Turn the pineapple upside down and leave it to stand for half an hour before cutting – this makes it juicier.

Energy 108kcal/461kJ; Protein 1.3g; Carbohydrate 26.1g, of which sugars 25.8g; Fat 0.6g, of which saturates 0.1g; Cholesterol 0mg; Calcium 55mg; Fibre 4.2g; Sodium 23mg.

Green juices

This chapter contains a selection of fabulous green juices that have wonderful health benefits. Highly nutritious, natural additives such as wheatgrass, spirulina, baobab, hemp and matcha are combined with all manner of everyday fruit and vegetables to make a range of feel-good drinks for the seriously health-conscious.

Citrus burst

Light and super-refreshing, this is tea but not as you know it. Grapefruit adds a slight sharpness that wakes you up in a far healthier way than a strong cup of tea or caffeine-loaded black coffee.

1 Press the grapefruit, orange and apple through the juicer, then press through the lettuce.

2 Pour the juice into a glass, add the matcha tea powder and fork together to combine.

Serves 1

1 white-fleshed grapefruit, peel and pith cut away

1 orange, peel and pith cut away

1 green apple, no need to peel or core

½ romaine lettuce

2.5ml/½ tsp matcha green tea powder

JUICE TIP – If you don't like grapefruit, you could use another orange, although the end result won't be as fresh-tasting and zingy.

Energy 94kcal/398kJ; Protein 2.7g; Carbohydrate 21.2g, of which sugars 21.2g; Fat 0.3g, of which saturates 0g; Cholesterol 0mg; Calcium 95mg; Fibre 1.0g; Sodium 11mg.

Pineapple pleaser

Serves 1

¼ medium pineapple, skin cut away but core left in, or 200g/7oz/1 cup prepared pineapple, cut into chunks

75g/3oz/¾ cup broccoli florets and sliced stem

75g/3oz or ½ courgette/zucchini

100g/3¾oz cucumber

pineapple slices, for stirrers (optional)

JUICE TIP – To get the maximum juice out of your pineapple store it at room temperature before cutting it. You can also turn it upside down half an hour before using it.

A light, refreshing frothy juice with just a hint of broccoli. Pineapple is low in calories at just 41 per 100g/3¾oz peeled weight, rich in vitamins A and C, and is a great source of essential minerals, manganese for energy production, potassium to help regulate heart rate and blood pressure, and copper for red blood synthesis.

1 Press the pineapple and all the vegetables through the juicer.

2 Pour into a tall glass. Add pineapple slice stirrers, if liked, and serve immediately.

Energy 135kcal/570kJ; Protein 6.6g; Carbohydrate 24.9g, of which sugars 24.4g; Fat 1.6g, of which saturates 0.2g; Cholesterol 0mg; Calcium 121mg; Fibre 0.7g; Sodium 14mg.

Wake-up call

Serves 1

25g/1oz/1 cup rocket/ arugula leaves

25g/1oz/1 cup baby spinach leaves

3 fresh mint stems

1 green apple, no need to peel or core

½ cucumber

75g/3oz/½ cup seedless green grapes

5ml/1 tsp baobab powder (optional)

NUTRIENT NOTE – Baobab powder can be bought from any good health food store. It is rich in probiotics as well as potassium, calcium, magnesium and vitamin C.

Awaken those tastebuds with this refreshing, zingy, pretty pale-green juice. Cucumber aids hydration, while the green grapes add natural sweetness and mint aids digestion.

1 Add the rocket leaves to the juicer chute then gradually press all the remaining ingredients through the juicer in order, except the baobab powder.

2 Whisk in the baobab powder, if using, until well blended. Pour the juice into a glass to serve.

Energy 94kcal/398kJ; Protein 2.7g; Carbohydrate 21.2g, of which sugars 21.2g; Fat 0.3g, of which saturates 0g; Cholesterol 0mg; Calcium 95mg; Fibre 1.0g; Sodium 11mg.

Broccoli body balancer

When on a detox, cutting out tea and coffee can be really hard. This refreshing juice makes a much healthier caffeine-free alternative and if you serve it with the spirulina stirred in you will be adding a protein power-boost too.

Serves 1

100g/3¾oz/1 cup broccoli florets and sliced stem

250g/9oz or 1½ courgettes/zucchini

1 apple, no need to peel or core

1cm/½in piece of fresh root ginger, no need to peel

2.5ml/½ tsp powdered spirulina (optional)

1 Press the vegetables, apple and ginger through the juicer.

2 Whisk the spirulina into the juice if using, then pour into a tall glass and serve.

JUICE TIP – When juicing fruits and vegetables, use the freshest ingredients you can find, for maximum flavour and nutrition.

Energy 109kcal/456kJ; Protein 9.2g; Carbohydrate 14.2g, of which sugars 13.7g; Fat 2g, of which saturates 0.5g; Cholesterol 0mg; Calcium 121mg; Fibre 0.8g; Sodium 13mg.

Gingered thirst quencher

Serves 1

½ romaine lettuce heart

½ cucumber

1cm/½in slice of fresh root ginger, no need to peel

5cm/2in piece of broccoli stem

1 celery stick

1 green apple, no need to peel or core

ice cubes

extra celery sticks, for stirrers (optional)

The perfect summery cocktail to enjoy with ice, this juice is light, delicate and refreshing with just a hint of ginger. Don't be tempted to be over-generous with the ginger or you will overpower the other flavours.

1 Gradually press all the ingredients through a juicer.

2 Pour into a tall tumbler half-filled with ice cubes and serve with celery stick stirrers, if liked.

JUICE TIP – As apples vary in size you may need to cut it in half, or even quarters to fit into the chute of your juicer. Make sure to serve this fresh juice immediately as the apple will oxidize and brown as it stands.

Energy 68kcal/282kJ; Protein 3.2g; Carbohydrate 11.8g, of which sugars 11.7g; Fat 1.1g, of which saturates 0.2g; Cholesterol 0mg; Calcium 68mg; Fibre 0.5g; Sodium 26mg.

Parslied purifier

Parsley has long been used in herbal medicine as a blood tonic and purifier, natural diuretic and as a digestive aid, and it may even help with bad breath.

1 Press the parsley through the juicer, followed gradually by the spinach, celery and apples.

2 Pour into one large or two small glasses and stir in the hemp oil.

Serves 1–2

15g/½oz/¾ cup fresh parsley

25g/1oz/1 cup baby spinach leaves

1 celery stick

2 green apples, no need to peel or core

5ml/1 tsp hemp oil

JUICE TIP – You don't get a lot of juice from parsley but what you do extract is a very deep green and adds a unique and delicate flavour.

Energy 111kcal/465kJ; Protein 1.9g; Carbohydrate 18.8g, of which sugars 18.7g; Fat 3.6g, of which saturates 0.5g; Cholesterol 0mg; Calcium 91mg; Fibre 0.7g; Sodium 63mg.

Wheatgrass tonic

Wheatgrass is a concentrated source of chlorophyll, which combats tiredness and fatigue, and also provides enzymes, vitamins and minerals.

1 Using a small, sharp knife, roughly shred the cabbage.

2 Press the cabbage through a juicer with the wheatgrass. Pour the juice into two small glasses and serve immediately.

Serves 2

50g/2oz white cabbage

90g/3½oz wheatgrass

JUICE TIP – Wheatgrass has a distinctive flavour so in this juice it is blended with mild white cabbage. It is just as tasty combined with other vegetables instead, so play around.

Energy 36kcal/149kJ; Protein 3.2g; Carbohydrate 3.9g, of which sugars 3.8g; Fat 0.8g, of which saturates 0.1g; Cholesterol 0mg; Calcium 178mg; Fibre 2.9g; Sodium 130mg.

Green goddess

Serves 1

1 kiwi fruit, no need to peel

225g/8oz or ¼ green-fleshed melon, seeded, peeled and cut into slices that will fit in the juicer chute

25g/1oz/1 cup baby spinach leaves

175g/6oz or 1 courgette/zucchini

JUICE TIP – Courgettes/zucchini make a great low-calorie addition to any juice and as their flavour is so mild they work with virtually any other fruit and vegetable. Juicing them is therefore a great way to use up a summer glut.

Having a stressful day? Don't reach for the chocolate bar or cookie jar. This delicately sweet and soothing juice is the perfect stressbuster and not only is it lower in calories but it is bursting with vitamins and minerals, too.

1 Gradually press all the ingredients through a juicer.

2 Pour into a tall glass and serve.

Energy 121kcal/509kJ; Protein 5.9g; Carbohydrate 22.3g, of which sugars 21.9g; Fat 1.4g, of which saturates 0.2g; Cholesterol 0mg; Calcium 133mg; Fibre 0.6g; Sodium 93mg.

Citrus super-cleanse

Reawaken those tastebuds with this fresh-tasting immune-boosting citrus juice. Grapefruit can be a little sharp but by mixing with orange and pear the freshness will be balanced with a little soothing and naturally sweet pear juice.

1 Press the kale into the juicer feeder chute, then gradually press all the other ingredients through the juicer.

2 Pour into a glass half-filled with ice cubes and serve.

Serves 1

25g/1oz/1 cup shredded kale

25g/1oz/1 cup baby spinach leaves

1 grapefruit, rind and pith cut away

1 orange, rind and pith cut away

½ pear, no need to peel or core

ice cubes

JUICE TIP - Cut the rind and most of the pith off citrus fruit before you juice or blend them. The coloured rind is just too strong-tasting and the pith can be bitter. The rind may also be coated in wax, which you don't want to drink!

Energy 94kcal/398kJ; Protein 2.7g; Carbohydrate 21.2g, of which sugars 21.2g; Fat 0.3g, of which saturates 0g; Cholesterol 0mg; Calcium 95mg; Fibre 1.0g; Sodium 11mg.

Mixed salad

As well as being full of water, lettuce and cucumber contain important minerals such as calcium and zinc, alongside other crucial nutrients like vitamin K. Spinach contains plenty of betacarotene and has cancer-fighting properties. Juiced with ripe pears for maximum sweetness, a regular dose of this super juice can only enhance your health.

Serves 2–3

½ cucumber

½ iceberg, cos or romaine lettuce

2 large, ripe pears, no need to peel or core

75g/3oz/3 cups baby spinach leaves

6–8 radishes

crushed ice

sliced radishes and cucumber, for stirrers

1 Using a small, sharp knife, chop the cucumber into chunks. Roughly tear the lettuce into pieces.

2 Press all the ingredients through a juicer.

3 Put crushed ice in two or three tall glasses, pour over the juice and serve with sliced radishes and cucumber for stirrers.

JUICE TIP - Although it can taste fairly bland in a salad, unpeeled cucumber has a surprisingly intense flavour when it is juiced. If you prefer a lighter taste, peel the cucumber with a sharp knife before juicing.

Energy 64kcal/270kJ; Protein 2.1g; Carbohydrate 12.9g, of which sugars 12.8g; Fat 0.7g, of which saturates 0.1g; Cholesterol 0mg; Calcium 88mg; Fibre 3.9g; Sodium 44mg.

Summer salad bowl

All the flavours of a summery salad in a glass. This super low-calorie drink has slightly peppery undertones with just a hint of celery; if you are a fan of a bloody Mary, you will love this. If not, you can use milder-tasting baby spinach leaves instead.

Serves 1–2

25g/1oz/1 cup rocket/arugula or baby spinach leaves

100g/3¾oz/generous ⅔ cup seedless green grapes

½ romaine lettuce, plus one or two leaves, for stirrers (optional)

¼ cucumber

1 celery stick

1 Press the rocket or spinach leaves into the feeder chute of the juicer, then gradually press the grapes, lettuce, cucumber and celery sticks through the juicer.

2 Pour into one or two glasses and serve, with lettuce leaf stirrers, if liked.

JUICE TIP – Celery has a surprisingly strong taste, even though it is primarily made up of water. If you are not a fan then simply leave it out and instead use a few broccoli florets or half a courgette/zucchini.

NUTRIENT NOTE – While most of us just tend to add rocket or arugula to a mixed leafy salad, it has so much more nutritionally than an average lettuce. Related to kale, it contains powerful antioxidants, and is an excellent source of vitamins C and K, as well as folates, copper and iron. Some even think it has aphrodisiac properties.

Energy 89kcal/376kJ; Protein 2.5g; Carbohydrate 18.7g, of which sugars 18.6g; Fat 1g, of which saturates 0.1g; Cholesterol 0mg; Calcium 85mg; Fibre 0.4g; Sodium 44mg.

Supergreen vitality

A thirst-quenching veggilicious juice rich in cancer-fighting antioxidants, vitamins and minerals but low in calories. The pear adds just a hint of natural sweetness to neutralize and balance the strong taste of kale.

1 Press the shredded or whole kale leaves into the feeder chute of the juicer, then gradually press the cucumber, celery sticks and pear through the juicer.

2 Add the lacuma and hemp powder and fork or whisk together until smooth. Pour into a tall glass and serve.

Serves 1

50g/2oz/2 cups shredded or whole kale leaves

½ cucumber

2 celery sticks

1 ripe pear, no need to peel or core

5ml/1 tsp lacuma powder

5ml/1 tsp hemp powder

JUICE TIP – Buy pears when they're a little hard and leave them to ripen in a fruit bowl in the kitchen so that the starch they contain turns to sugar, adding flavour. They contain about 70 calories depending on their size.

Energy 96kcal/402kJ; Protein 3.5g; Carbohydrate 18.5g, of which sugars 18.3g; Fat 1.2g, of which saturates 0.1g; Cholesterol 0mg; Calcium 133mg; Fibre 0.5g; Sodium 66mg.

Sugar snap

Sweet and juicy sugar snap peas are one of the most delicious vegetables to serve raw and they taste just as good when put through a juicer. The sweetness of the peas and the melon intensifies when they are juiced and the fresh root ginger adds a certain edge to this mellow, cooling juice. Keep the melon in the fridge so that it's well chilled when you come to blend the juice – you won't need to add ice.

Serves 1

1cm/½in piece of fresh root ginger, no need to peel

225g/8oz or ¼ honeydew or Galia melon

200g/7oz sugar snap peas

melon chunks and peas, to decorate

1 Using a sharp knife, chop the ginger. Scoop out the seeds from the melon and cut it into wedges. Cut away the skin, then chop the flesh into chunks.

2 Press the sugar snap peas through a juicer, followed by the chunks of melon and the slices of ginger.

3 Serve chilled, decorated with melon chunks and peas.

JUICE TIP – Use a fresh, plump-looking piece of ginger. If it is too old, it may have started to shrivel and won't produce the necessary juice and flavour.

Celery sensation

Savoury, almost salty, celery and sweet, green grapes make an astoundingly effective twosome when combined in a blended juice. A small handful of peppery watercress adds extra punch, but be careful not to add too much because its flavour intensifies considerably when the leaves are juiced. Celery has one of the lowest calorie contents of all vegetables, so this is a particularly useful juice for anyone on a low-calorie diet.

Serves 1

2 celery sticks

25g/1oz/1 cup watercress

200g/7oz/1¾ cups seedless green grapes

1 leafy celery stick, for a stirrer

crushed ice

1 Press the celery sticks through a juicer, followed by the watercress and the green grapes.

2 Put a leafy celery stick in a large glass to act as an edible swizzle stick and half-fill the glass with crushed ice. Pour the juice over the ice and serve.

Sugar snap: Energy 112kcal/476kJ; Protein 8.2g; Carbohydrate 19.6g, of which sugars 18g; Fat 0.6g, of which saturates 0g; Cholesterol 0mg; Calcium 114mg; Fibre 5.4g; Sodium 66mg

Celery: Energy 135kcal/579kJ; Protein 2.6g; Carbohydrate 31.5g, of which sugars 31.5g; Fat 0.8g, of which saturates 0.1g; Cholesterol 0mg; Calcium 136mg; Fibre 2.8g; Sodium 65mg.

Bean good

Serves 2

90g/3½oz broccoli

1 pear, no need to peel or core

90g/3½oz/scant ½ cup beansprouts

200g/7oz/1¾ cups seedless green grapes

ice cubes and sliced green grapes

NUTRIENT NOTE – Beansprouts are highly nutritious, bursting with vitamins B and C. They are also one of the few vegetables that increase in goodness after being picked.

Although mild in flavour, the juiciness of beansprouts works well in any nourishing blend. Mixed with broccoli, another superfood, and naturally sweet fruits, this blend is a real tonic for your skin, hair and general health.

1 Using a small, sharp knife cut the broccoli into florets small enough to fit through a juicer funnel.

2 Press all the ingredients through the juicer.

3 Pour into two short glasses and serve with ice cubes and sliced green grapes.

Energy 119kcal/505kJ; Protein 3.9g; Carbohydrate 25.5g, of which sugars 24.6g; Fat 0.8g, of which saturates 0.2g; Cholesterol 0mg; Calcium 56mg; Fibre 2.2g; Sodium 10mg.

Broccoli booster

Serves 1

125g/4¼oz/1¼ cups broccoli florets

2 eating apples, no need to peel or core

15ml/1 tbsp lemon juice

ice cubes

Hailed as a cure-all superfood and a vital ingredient in a healthy diet, broccoli's strong taste does need a bit of toning down when juiced. Sweet and tangy apples and lemon juice soften its flavour perfectly.

1 Press the broccoli and apple through a juicer, then stir in the lemon juice.

2 Serve in a tall glass with plenty of ice.

Energy 111kcal/475kJ; Protein 6.1g; Carbohydrate 20.1g, of which sugars 19.7g; Fat 1.3g, of which saturates 0.3g; Cholesterol 0mg; Calcium 78mg; Fibre 6.5g; Sodium 14mg.

Broccoli and watercress spritzer

Serves 1–2

25g/1oz/1 cup watercress

225g/8oz or ¼ green-fleshed melon, seeded, peeled and cut into slices that will fit in the juicer shoot

1cm/½in piece of fresh root ginger, no need to peel

½ pear, no need to peel or core

75g/3oz/¾ cup broccoli florets and sliced stem

125ml/4fl oz/½ cup sparkling mineral water, chilled

This super-vitality juice is packed with essential nutrients and natural fruit pectin to help cleanse and soothe the digestive system. Healthy, low-calorie and tastes good too.

1 Press the watercress into the feeder chute of the juicer, then gradually press the melon, ginger, pear and broccoli through the juicer.

2 Pour into tall glasses and top up with sparkling mineral water.

JUICE TIP – Often overshadowed by trendier rocket/arugula, watercress is high in bone-building and strengthening vitamin K and vitamin A, which is important for eye health. It also contains flavonoid antioxidants carotene, lutein and zeaxanthin, which not only support good vision but also benefit the cardiovascular system and help protect cells from free-radical damage.

NUTRIENT NOTE – The skin reflects what is going on inside the body; if we are stressed or run down, our skin will look tired and lifeless. A healthy juice is like giving your body a facial from the inside out.

Energy 112kcal/474kJ; Protein 5.3g; Carbohydrate 21.3g, of which sugars 21.1g; Fat 1.1g, of which saturates 0.2g; Cholesterol 0mg; Calcium 107mg; Fibre 0.7g; Sodium 70mg.

Zingy refresher

The high levels of chlorophyll in spirulina transforms this mid-green juice into the most dramatic dark green. It's rich in protein and vitamin B12 – a vitamin that can be difficult to obtain in sufficient amounts if you follow a vegan or vegetarian diet – plus calcium and iron.

1 Add the spinach to the juicer then gradually press all the fruit and vegetables through the juicer in order.

2 Add the spirulina powder to the juice to taste, and whisk together until smooth. Pour into a glass and serve.

Serves 1

50g/2oz/2 cups baby spinach leaves

¼ medium pineapple, skin cut away, core left in, halved lengthways

½ cucumber

2 celery sticks

5cm/2in piece of broccoli stalk

1.5–2.5ml/¼–½ tsp spirulina powder

JUICE TIPS

- Don't throw broccoli stems away; keep them to add to green juices. They have just as many nutrients as the florets.
- Sold in powdered form, spirulina makes a handy superfood booster for refreshing and thirst-quenching drinks.

Energy 117kcal/496kJ; Protein 4.3g; Carbohydrate 23.5g, of which sugars 23.3g; Fat 1.2g, of which saturates 0.1g; Cholesterol 0mg; Calcium 178mg; Fibre 1.2g; Sodium 115mg.

All-green pep-up

Serves 1

75g/3oz or 2 dark outer green Savoy cabbage leaves

175g/6oz or 1 courgette/zucchini

100g/3¾oz/generous ⅔ cup seedless green grapes

1 pear, no need to peel or core

1 green apple, no need to peel or core

5ml/1 tsp chia seeds

JUICE TIP - Homemade pear and apple juice quickly turns brown as it stands so make sure you serve this juice the minute that it is made. Since this one is made with added chia seeds, it will also thicken quite a lot if it is left to stand.

A super-vitality juice with plenty of essential nutrients and natural fruit pectin to help cleanse and settle the digestive system. The flavour of the cabbage is disguised by naturally sweet and soothing fruits, making it very palatable.

1 Roll the cabbage leaves up and feed them through the chute of the juicer, then add the courgette, grapes, pear and apple.

2 Pour the juice into a tall glass, stir in the chia seeds until well blended, then serve immediately.

Energy 226kcal/952kJ; Protein 6.9g; Carbohydrate 44.6g, of which sugars 44.2g; Fat 3.1g, of which saturates 0.5g; Cholesterol 0mg; Calcium 141mg; Fibre 1.4g; Sodium 64mg.

Apple and parsnip soother

Serves 1

2 green apples, no need to peel or core

75g/3oz or 1 small parsnip, scrubbed

25g/1oz/1 cup baby spinach leaves

75g/3oz or 3 florets cut from a green Romanesco cauliflower

a pinch of ground turmeric

JUICE TIP – Parsnips are at their sweetest a few weeks after the first frost of winter as the cold causes the starch they contain to turn to sugar.

NUTRIENT NOTE – Long used in natural medicine in China and India, turmeric is a natural antiseptic and antibacterial agent. Fresh turmeric root is now more widely available in supermarkets and Indian supermarkets – cut a slice and add to the juicer in much the same way as root ginger.

Soothe and calm your digestive system and boost immunity to help fight those winter cold germs with this sweet, earthy shot of superfood-packed juice.

1 Press all the ingredients through a juicer except the turmeric, then pour into a glass.

2 Stir in the turmeric and serve.

Energy 150kcal/634kJ; Protein 5.4g; Carbohydrate 29.7g, of which sugars 24.2g; Fat 1.8g, of which saturates 0.3g; Cholesterol 0mg; Calcium 95mg; Fibre 0.5g; Sodium 54mg.

Green bone builder

Serves 1–3

15g/½oz/½ cup watercress

25g/1oz/1 cup shredded kale

75g/3oz/¾ cup broccoli florets and sliced stem

1 pear, unpeeled and cored

1 orange, rind and pith cut away

90ml/6 tbsp plain low-fat or non-dairy yogurt

NUTRIENT NOTE – Vitamin D aids the absorption of bone-building calcium, and can be produced by the action of the sunlight on our body; the amount depends on how strong the sunlight is and whether or not you are in direct sunshine or in the shade, just 10–20 minutes outside a day is all it takes. Vitamin D is also added to many non-dairy milks.

Your skeleton doesn't actually stop growing until you are 21. Dairy foods, fortified milks and green leafy vegetables all help maintain bone strength and health. Whatever your age, regular exercise as well as a healthy diet is important to improve bone strength, muscle tone and especially for seniors, balance.

1 Press the watercress and kale through the juicer then add the broccoli, pear and orange.

2 Pour the juice into a glass or glasses and spoon in the yogurt. Stir lightly for a marbled effect then serve.

Energy 191kcal/811kJ; Protein 10.7g; Carbohydrate 33.7g, of which sugars 33.5g; Fat 2.4g, of which saturates 0.8g; Cholesterol 1mg; Calcium 319mg; Fibre 1.1g; Sodium 91mg.

Breakfast smoothies

Breakfast is often considered to be the most important meal of the day but its also often the most neglected, so give yourself a kick-start with these fuel-packed, imaginative drinks. Made in minutes and easier to digest than a bowl of cereal or a piece of toast, fabulous fresh smoothies provide the perfect early-morning boost.

Big breakfast

Easy to prepare and even easier to drink, this energy-packed smoothie makes a great start to the day. Bananas and sesame seeds provide the perfect fuel in the form of slow-release carbohydrate that will keep you going all morning, while fresh and zesty orange juice and sweet, scented mango set your tastebuds tingling first thing.

1 Using a small, sharp knife, skin the mango, then slice the flesh off the pit. Peel the banana and break it into short lengths, then place it in a blender goblet with the mango.

2 Squeeze the juice from the orange and add to the blender goblet with the bran, sesame seeds and honey. Screw on the lid and blitz until smooth, then pour into two glasses and serve.

Serves 2

½ mango
1 banana
1 large orange
30ml/2 tbsp wheat bran
15ml/1 tbsp sesame seeds
10–15ml/2–3 tsp honey

SMOOTHIE TIP – Mango juice is naturally very sweet so you may wish to add less honey or leave it out altogether.

Energy 123kcal/523kJ; Protein 3.4g; Carbohydrate 26.9g, of which sugars 23.7g; Fat 1g, of which saturates 0.2g; Cholesterol 0mg; Calcium 40mg; Fibre 3.6g; Sodium 5mg..

Muesli smoothie

Serves 2

1 piece of preserved stem ginger, plus 30ml/2 tbsp syrup from the ginger jar

50g/2oz/¼ cup ready-to-eat dried apricots, halved or quartered

40g/1½oz/scant ½ cup natural muesli or granola

about 200ml/7fl oz/scant 1 cup semi-skimmed/low-fat milk

SMOOTHIE TIP – Apricot and ginger are perfect partners in this divine drink. It makes an incredibly healthy, tasty breakfast, but is so delicious and indulgent that you could even serve it as a dessert after a summer meal.

Another good breakfast booster, this store-cupboard smoothie can be a lifesaver if you've run out of fresh fruit. It's also an option for breakfast in bed without the crumbs. Any extra drink can be covered and stored overnight in the fridge, although you'll need to add more milk in the morning as it will thicken on standing.

1 Chop the preserved ginger and put it in a blender goblet with the syrup, apricots, muesli and milk.

2 Screw on the lid and process the mixture until smooth, adding more milk if necessary. Serve in two wide glasses.

Energy 203kcal/862kJ; Protein 6.4g; Carbohydrate 40.1g, of which sugars 30.9g; Fat 3.2g, of which saturates 1.3g; Cholesterol 6mg; Calcium 163mg; Fibre 2.9g; Sodium 163mg.

Vitamin C supercharge

Rich in vitamin C, berries and kale help the white blood cells fight infections, so boosting immunity. And if that isn't enough, they help to keep our skin youthful by producing collagen, a protein that maintains the skin's elasticity.

Serves 1

25g/1oz/1 cup shredded kale

50g/2oz/½ cup blueberries

75g/3oz or about 3 large strawberries, hulled, halved or quartered

115g/4oz/½ cup low-fat plain yogurt or non-dairy alternative

15ml/1 tbsp ground seed mix, see below

125ml/4fl oz/½ cup water, or to taste

1 Put all the ingredients in a blender goblet, screw on the lid and blitz until smooth and frothy.

2 Stir in a little extra water if needed, then pour the smoothie into a tall glass.

SMOOTHIE TIP – Choose fresh berries in summer when their flavour is at its best. During the winter months when prices are high, frozen berries make a great standby; just take out as many as and when you need them, and blitz while still frozen.

NUTRIENT NOTE – Blueberries are naturally sweet but contain just 57 calories per 100g/3¾oz. They are packed with nutrients – vitamins C, A and E – which together work as potent antioxidants, plus phenol compounds and fibre for optimum health.

GROUND SEED MIX

Makes about 125g/4¼oz/ generous 1 cup

45ml/3 tbsp sesame seeds

45ml/3 tbsp sunflower seeds

45ml/3 tbsp pumpkin seeds

45ml/3 tbsp golden flaxseeds

1 Measure the seeds into a blender goblet or spice mill and blitz until finely ground.

2 Scoop out and store in a sealed plastic container in the fridge for up to 2 weeks.

Smoothie: Energy 209kcal/875kJ; Protein 9.9g; Carbohydrate 23.8g, of which sugars 19g; Fat 8.9g, of which saturates 1.8g; Cholesterol 2mg; Calcium 247mg; Fibre 4.9g; Sodium 89mg.
Seeds: Energy 177kcal/758kJ; Protein 4.8g; Carbohydrate 38.1g, of which sugars 37.8g; Fat 1.8g, of which saturates 0.5g; Cholesterol 0mg; Calcium 142mg; Fibre 8.6g; Sodium 158mg.

Gazpacho pep-up

Serves 2

½ fresh red chilli

800g/1¾lb tomatoes, skinned

½ cucumber, roughly sliced

1 red bell pepper, seeded and cut into chunks

1 celery stick, chopped

1 spring onion/scallion, roughly chopped

25g/1oz/1 cup fresh coriander/ cilantro, stalks included, plus extra to decorate

juice of 1 lime

a pinch of salt

ice cubes

Inspired by the classic Spanish soup, this fabulous smoothie looks and tastes delicious and is a great way to wake up your tastebuds. Fresh salad vegetables can be thrown into a blender goblet and whizzed up in moments to create a refreshing, invigorating drink. If you are planning to invite friends for a relaxing al fresco lunch, serve this cooling smoothie as an appetizer.

1 Using a sharp knife, seed the chilli. Add to a blender goblet with the tomatoes, cucumber, red pepper, celery, spring onion and fresh coriander.

2 Screw on the lid and blend well until smooth, scraping the mixture down from the sides of the goblet, if necessary.

3 Add the lime juice and a pinch of salt and blend. Pour into two glasses. Add ice cubes and fresh coriander leaves to serve.

SMOOTHIE TIPS

- Stir in a little extra tomato juice or mineral water if the smoothie is still thick after blending. A splash of red wine vinegar will intensify the flavour.
- Drinks made from fresh salad vegetables, packed full of valuable nutrients, are the ultimate thirst quenchers on a hot day, providing wonderfully fresh flavours and refreshing the palate instantly.

Energy 32kcal/137kJ; Protein 1.5g; Carbohydrate 5.7g, of which sugars 5.6g; Fat 0.5g, of which saturates 0.2g; Cholesterol 0mg; Calcium 22mg; Fibre 1.9g; Sodium 19mg.

Good morning shake

Boost energy levels with naturally sweet high-fibre fruits rather than processed sugary breakfast cereals. There is strong evidence that the natural pectin (the substance that helps jam to set) found in the soluble fibre of pears and apples can help to lower cholesterol in the blood and to slow down the rate at which glucose is absorbed.

1 Put all the ingredients in a blender goblet, screw on the lid and blitz until smooth.

2 Pour into one tall glass or two short glasses to serve.

Serves 1–2

10 unblanched almonds

15ml/1 tbsp pumpkin seeds

15ml/1 tbsp unflavoured pea protein or hemp powder

1 ripe pear, quartered, cored, but not peeled, cut into chunks

100g/3¾oz/generous ⅔ cup seedless green grapes

25g/1oz/1 cup shredded kale

175ml/6fl oz/¾ cup coconut water from a carton

SMOOTHIE TIP – Pea protein powder or hemp powder is a great way for those on a vegan diet to boost protein levels. Buy a plain or flavoured type from a health food store.

NUTRIENT NOTE – Almonds are an easy way to provide protein in a shake and for those on a vegetarian diet are good for boosting those vitamins and minerals usually found in animal sources. The unsaturated fats they contain also boost energy.

Energy 573kcal/2393kJ; Protein 28.2g; Carbohydrate 37g, of which sugars 33g; Fat 35.6g, of which saturates 3.3g; Cholesterol 0mg; Calcium 188mg; Fibre 7.9g; Sodium 27mg.

Swiss mix

Serves 1

15ml/1 tbsp rolled oats

6 unblanched almonds

15ml/1 tbsp sunflower seeds

15ml/1 tbsp dried goji berries

5ml/1 tsp wheatgrass powder

1 kiwi fruit, peeled and into chunks

½ pear, no need to peel, cut into chunks

25g/1oz/1 cup shredded kale

250ml/8fl oz/1 cup unsweetened oat milk

SMOOTHIE TIP – Use unsweetened nut, coconut, pea or rice milk instead of oat milk, if liked.

All the flavours of a classic Bircher muesli mixed with goji berries, wheatgrass and kale for a modern twist on a favourite healthy breakfast.

1 Put all the ingredients in a blender goblet, screw on the lid and blitz until smooth.

2 Pour into a glass and serve.

NUTRIENT NOTE – Goji berries are now widely available in supermarkets and health food stores. They are rich in carotenes, which help to boost our immune system, and some research suggests that regular consumption may protect against heart disease and cancer.

Energy 653kcal/1918kJ; Protein 12.4g; Carbohydrate 42.7g, of which sugars 33.9g; Fat 20.7g, of which saturates 1.7g; Cholesterol 0mg; Calcium 116mg; Fibre 7.7g; Sodium 23mg.

Cauliflower jumpstart

Cauliflowers are back in fashion and high on the superfood list as they contain vitamins, minerals, antioxidants and phytochemicals. While they may not be the obvious choice for a shake-style drink, they add a creamy smoothness that combines with the natural sweetness of the banana and earthy flavour of the mushroom tea in this energizing breakfast-boosting combo.

Serves 1

1 sachet or 5ml/1 tsp powdered instant chaga mushroom tea

50ml/2fl oz/¼ cup boiling water

¼ small cauliflower with a few tiny attached leaves, cut into chunks

1 small banana, peeled and cut into chunks

75g/3oz or ½ courgette/zucchini, sliced

25g/1oz/1 cup baby spinach leaves

50g/2oz/½ cup broccoli florets

175ml/6fl oz/½ cup cold water

5ml/1 tsp maple syrup or sweetener of your choice

1 Put the mushroom tea powder and boiling water in a cup and mix together until all the powder has dissolved.

2 Pour the mushroom tea into a blender goblet, then add the cauliflower, banana, courgette, baby spinach leaves and broccoli. Pour in the water, screw on the lid and blitz until smooth and frothy.

3 Stir in the maple syrup or sweetener of choice to taste, then pour into a glass to serve.

SMOOTHIE TIP – This is a thick shake, so adjust the consistency with a little ice or extra water, if preferred.

Energy 168kcal/705kJ; Protein 9.7g; Carbohydrate 28.3g, of which sugars 25.3g; Fat 2.3g, of which saturates 0.5g; Cholesterol 0mg; Calcium 124mg; Fibre 7.5g; Sodium 52mg.

Cacao comforter

Serves 1

10ml/2 tsp raw cacao powder

a pinch of ground cinnamon

250ml/8fl oz/1 cup unsweetened almond milk

50g/2oz or 2 cauliflower florets

25g/1oz/1 cup shredded kale

25g/1oz or 1 large date, pitted

½ banana, peeled and chopped

You don't need to miss out on a chocolate fix when trying to eat in a healthier way. This super-filling, energy-boosting meal in a glass will sustain you until lunchtime. Mixing raw cacao powder with kale is a good way to tempt sceptics who claim that kale isn't for them.

1 Put all the ingredients in a blender goblet, screw on the lid and blitz until smooth and frothy.

2 Adjust the consistency with a little water or extra almond milk if needed, then pour into a tall glass to serve.

SMOOTHIE TIP – Unsweetened almond milk has been suggested in this recipe but rice milk or oat milk would also work just as well. They are all fortified with extra calcium, vitamin B12 and vitamin D, plus they are low in fat and lactose free, although calorie counts vary slightly.

Energy 242kcal/1023kJ; Protein 6.5g; Carbohydrate 47.7g, of which sugars 44.7g; Fat 4.2g, of which saturates 0.8g; Cholesterol 0mg; Calcium 65mg; Fibre 5.7g; Sodium 223mg.

Banana booster

Bananas are a great energy food. They are packed with valuable nutrients and healthy carbohydrates, and they also fill you up, which is definitely a bonus. Blended with the additional fruits – pineapple, dates and lemon juice – and creamy milk, this delectable concoction will keep you going for hours. If you're prone to snacking throughout the day, try this and you'll feel all the better for it. Any leftover drink can be stored in the fridge for up to a day.

Serves 2–3

½ pineapple

4 Medjool dates, pitted

1 small banana

juice of 1 lemon

300ml/½ pint/1¼ cups very cold full-fat/whole milk or non-dairy milk

1 Cut away the skin and core from the pineapple. Chop the flesh and put it in a blender goblet, then add the dates.

2 Peel and chop the banana and add it to the rest of the fruit together with the lemon juice.

3 Screw on the lid and blend until smooth, scraping the mixture down from the sides of the goblet, if necessary. Add the milk and process briefly until well combined. Pour the smoothie into two or three glasses and serve immediately.

Zesty soya smoothie

Whizzed up with freshly squeezed orange juice, a splash of tangy lemon and a little honey, tofu can be transformed into a drink that's smooth, creamy, nutritious and delicious. Most people would not think to add tofu to a blended drink, but please do try it – you will be genuinely surprised. If possible, try to get hold of some silken tofu for this smoothie, as it has a wonderful satiny texture that blends particularly well.

Serves 1

2 oranges

15ml/1 tbsp lemon juice

20–25ml/4–5 tsp sunflower honey or herb honey

150g/5oz silken tofu

long, thin strips of pared orange rind, to decorate

1 Finely grate the rind of one orange and set aside. Juice both oranges and pour the juice into a blender goblet. Add the orange rind, lemon juice, sunflower or herb honey and tofu.

2 Screw on the lid and blitz until smooth and creamy, then pour into a glass. Decorate with the pared orange rind and serve.

Banana: Energy 187kcal/793kJ; Protein 4.7g; Carbohydrate 34.6g, of which sugars 34g; Fat 4.3g, of which saturates 2.5g; Cholesterol 14mg; Calcium 152mg; Fibre 2.5g; Sodium 48mg.
Soya: Energy 350kcal/1483kJ; Protein 15.6g; Carbohydrate 60.9g, of which sugars 60.3g; Fat 6.6g, of which saturates 0.8g; Cholesterol 0mg; Calcium 908mg; Fibre 5.1g; Sodium 26mg.

Sweet dream

Serves 2

25g/1oz/scant ¼ cup dates, pitted

50g/2oz/¼ cup ready-to-eat prunes

25g/1oz/scant ¼ cup sultanas/golden raisins

1 grapefruit

350ml/12fl oz/1½ cups full-fat/whole milk

30ml/2 tbsp Greek/strained plain yogurt

SMOOTHIE TIP – For a lighter version of this drink, omit the yogurt; the consistency of the smoothie will not be as creamy but it will still be delicious. You can also use your favourite kind of non-dairy yogurt and plant milk instead of dairy milk.

A soothing blend guaranteed to wake you up slowly, this fruity threesome is naturally sweet so there is no need for any additional sugar. Fresh grapefruit juice marries brilliantly with the dried fruits, and rich, creamy yogurt makes a delicious contrast of colour and flavour.

1 Put the fruits in a blender goblet. Squeeze the grapefruit juice and add to the goblet. Screw on the lid and blend until smooth, scraping down from the sides if necessary. Add the milk and blend until smooth.

2 Using a teaspoon, tap a spoonful of the yogurt around the inside of each of two glasses. Pour in the fruit mixture and serve.

Energy 246kcal/1033kJ; Protein 8.6g; Carbohydrate 38.3g, of which sugars 38.3g; Fat 7.4g, of which saturates 4.5g; Cholesterol 25mg; Calcium 301mg; Fibre 3.7g; Sodium 103mg.

Pear pep-up

This nutritious blend of ripe, juicy fruit, wheatgerm, yogurt, seeds and watercress makes a great-tasting thick and satisfying smoothie to get your morning going.

1 Roughly chop the watercress (you do not need to remove the tough stalks). Peel, core and roughly chop the pear.

2 Put the watercress and pear in a blender goblet with the wheatgerm and blend until smooth. Add the yogurt, flaxseeds and lemon juice. Screw on the lid and blend until smooth.

3 Thin with mineral water if the mixture is too thick. Pour into a glass over ice cubes and top with watercress.

Serves 1

25g/1oz/1 cup watercress, plus extra, to decorate

1 large ripe pear

30ml/2 tbsp wheatgerm

150ml/¼ pint/⅔ cup natural/plain yogurt

15ml/1 tbsp flaxseeds

10ml/2 tsp lemon juice

mineral water (optional)

ice cubes

SMOOTHIE TIP – If you never have time for breakfast, prepare this smoothie in the evening and chill it overnight. You can drink the smoothie on your journey into work and you'll then feel the benefits kick in throughout the day.

Energy 346kcal/1454kJ; Protein 19.6g; Carbohydrate 39.9g, of which sugars 31.2g; Fat 13.4g, of which saturates 2.5g; Cholesterol 2mg; Calcium 461mg; Fibre 3.5g; Sodium 146mg.

Late breakfast

Serves 2

250g/9oz firm tofu

200g/7oz/1¾ cups strawberries

45ml/3 tbsp pumpkin or sunflower seeds, plus extra for sprinkling

30–45ml/2–3 tbsp clear honey

juice of 2 large oranges

juice of 1 lemon

This energizing blend is just what you need when the morning has got off to a slow start. Not only is tofu a perfect source of protein, but it is also rich in minerals and contains nutrients that protect against dangerous diseases.

1 Roughly chop the tofu, then hull and roughly chop the strawberries. Reserve a few strawberry chunks for decoration.

2 Put all the ingredients in a blender goblet. Screw on the lid and blend until smooth, scraping down from the sides if necessary. Pour into glasses and sprinkle with extra seeds and the reserved strawberry chunks.

Energy 310kcal/1296kJ; Protein 15.7g; Carbohydrate 26.9g, of which sugars 22.6g; Fat 16.1g, of which saturates 1.7g; Cholesterol 0mg; Calcium 684mg; Fibre 2.5g; Sodium 19mg.

Golden wonder

Ripe plums make delicious juices and work really well with the banana and passion fruit in this unconventional blend. Use yellow plums if you can find them, as they are irresistibly sweet and juicy, but red ones can easily be substituted as long as they're soft and ripe. Vitamin-rich and energizing, this drink is sure to set you up for the day.

Serves 1–2

2 passion fruit
2 yellow plums
1 banana, peeled and sliced
about 15ml/1 tbsp lemon juice

1 Halve the passion fruit and scoop the pulp into a blender goblet. Halve and pit the plums and add to the blender goblet, along with the banana and lemon juice.

2 Screw on the lid and blend until smooth, scraping down from the sides if necessary. Pour into one large glass ot two small ones, and check the sweetness. Add more lemon juice, if you like.

SMOOTHIE TIP – If you prefer a juice without seeds, press the passion fruit pulp through a small sieve or strainer before adding the juice to the blender goblet and blitzing.

Energy 108kcal/461kJ; Protein 2.1g; Carbohydrate 25.6g, of which sugars 23.7g; Fat 0.4g, of which saturates 0.1g; Cholesterol 0mg; Calcium 16mg; Fibre 2.8g; Sodium 8mg.

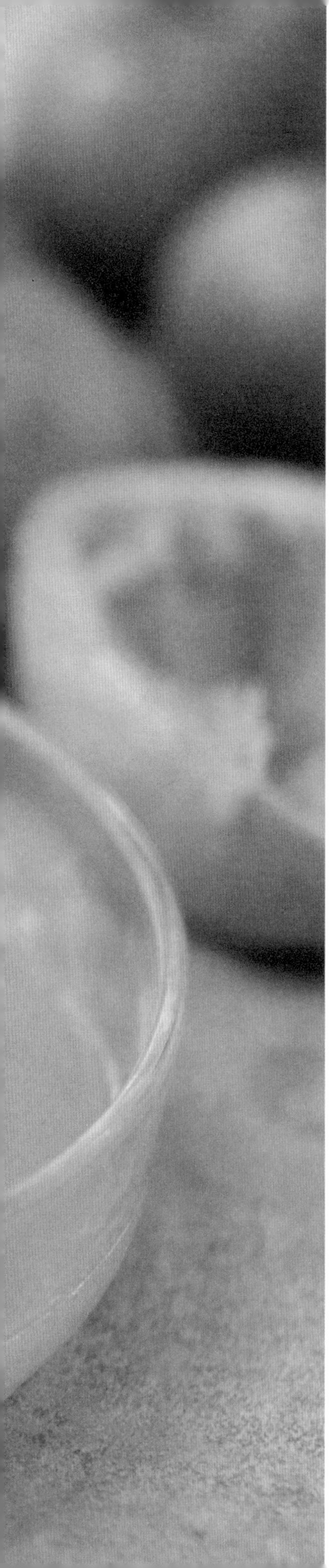

Fruity smoothies

Refreshingly tangy or as smooth as silk, super smoothies have earned their place as one of our favourite drinks. Keep them simple with pure fruit blends, or try something a little different by adding coconut cream, fruit tea, herbs or spices. Let the ideas in this irresistible chapter inspire you to experiment with all kinds of combinations.

Tropical fruit smoothie

Sweet, fruity and packed with vitamin C, this smoothie is a brilliant way to get children to enjoy healthy drinks. If you use really ripe fruit, it shouldn't need any additional sweetening, but taste it to check before serving. Mango makes a thick purée when blended, so top it up with water.

1 Cut away the skin from half a pineapple, discard the core and chop the flesh. Put the pieces of pineapple in a blender goblet with the grapes. Halve the mango either side of the flat pit. Scoop all the flesh into the blender.

2 Screw on the lid and process until really smooth, scraping the mixture down from the sides of the goblet if necessary.

3 Pour into two glasses and top up with water, if using. Serve.

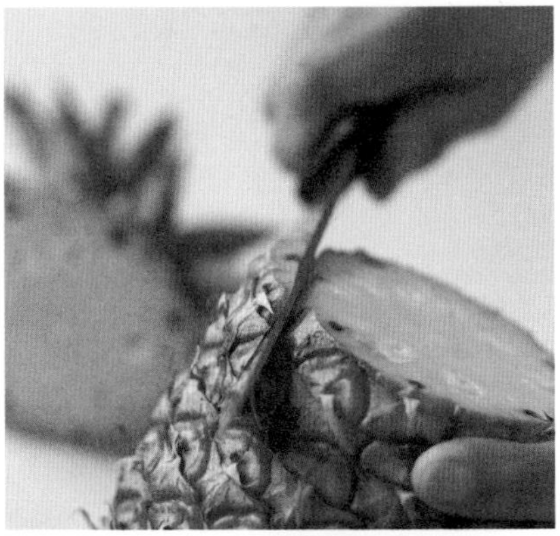

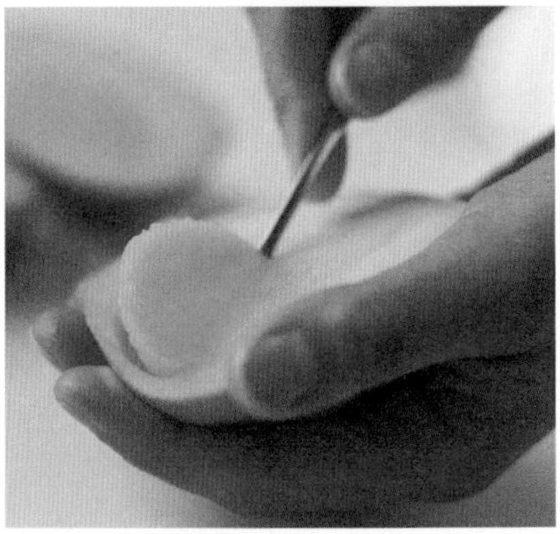

Serves 2

½ small pineapple

90g/3½oz/⅔ cup seedless white grapes

1 mango

mineral water (optional)

SMOOTHIE TIP – To make a novelty decoration, thread pieces of fruit on to paper straws or cocktail sticks and add them to the glasses before you serve the smoothies.

Energy 129kcal/553kJ; Protein 1.3g; Carbohydrate 32.3g, of which sugars 32g; Fat 0.4g, of which saturates 0.1g; Cholesterol 0mg; Calcium 37mg; Fibre 3.7g; Sodium 5mg.

Orange and raspberry smoothie

Serves 2–3

250g/9oz/1⅓ cups raspberries, chilled

200ml/7fl oz/scant 1 cup natural/plain yogurt, chilled

300ml/½ pint/1¼ cups freshly squeezed orange juice, chilled

SMOOTHIE TIP – For a super-chilled version you can use frozen raspberries instead of fresh. You may need to blend the raspberries and yogurt for a little longer to get a really smooth result.

This exquisite blend combines the sharp-sweet taste of raspberries and the refreshing fruitiness of oranges with smooth yogurt. It tastes like creamy, fruit heaven in a glass. Even better, it takes just minutes to prepare.

1 Place the raspberries and yogurt in a blender goblet, screw on the lid and process for about 1 minute until smooth and creamy.

2 Add the orange juice to the raspberry and yogurt mixture and process for another 30 seconds or until thoroughly combined.

3 Pour into two or three tall glasses and serve immediately.

Energy 94kcal/401kJ; Protein 5.1g; Carbohydrate 17.6g, of which sugars 17.6g; Fat 1g, of which saturates 0.4g; Cholesterol 1mg; Calcium 158mg; Fibre 2.2g; Sodium 68mg.

Immune zoom

Orange-coloured fruits and vegetables are particularly good for protecting against or fighting off colds or flu, and are full of powerful antioxidants. This refreshing, fruity drink also contains a herbal blend called echinacea, which may help to relieve the symptoms of colds and flu.

1 Halve the mango, cutting down one side of the flat pit. Remove the pit and scoop the flesh from the skin. Roughly chop the flesh and place it in a blender goblet.

2 Peel, core and chop the apple. Add to the blender, screw on the lid and blitz until smooth, scraping down from the sides if necessary.

3 Halve the passion fruit and scoop the pulp into the mango and apple purée. Add the orange juice and echinacea, then blend briefly. Thin with a little mineral water, if you like, then pour into two glasses and serve.

Serves 2

1 small mango
1 eating apple
2 passion fruit
juice of 1 orange
5ml/1 tsp echinacea
mineral water (optional)
ice cubes (optional)

SMOOTHIE TIP – Echinacea can be taken to help treat or ward off a cold. Make sure you check the recommended dosage on the manufacturer's packaging before use.

Ginseng smoother

Ginseng is a natural cure-all that is claimed to stimulate digestion, reduce tiredness, alleviate stress, strengthen the immune system and even revive a flagging libido. Here it is added to the juice as a powder but it can also be taken as a dietary supplement in tablet form.

1 Remove the core from the pepper and roughly chop the flesh. Slice the pumpkin in half. Scoop out the seeds with a spoon and then cut away the skin. Chop the flesh. Halve and pit the apricot.

2 Push the pumpkin through a juicer. Put the pepper and apricot in a blender goblet with the pumpkin juice, screw on the lid and blitz until smooth. Add a squeeze of lemon juice and the ginseng powder, and stir to combine. Pour the juice over ice cubes in a tall glass and serve.

Serves 1

1 red or orange bell pepper
200g/7oz pumpkin
1 large apricot
squeeze of lemon juice
5ml/1 tsp ginseng powder
ice cubes

Immune: Energy 69kcal/296kJ; Protein 1.2g; Carbohydrate 16.7g, of which sugars 16.4g; Fat 0.3g, of which saturates 0.1g; Cholesterol 0mg; Calcium 15mg; Fibre 0.5g; Sodium 8mg.

Ginseng: Energy 94kcal/398kJ; Protein 3.5g; Carbohydrate 18.5g, of which sugars 17g; Fat 1.1g, of which saturates 0.4g; Cholesterol 0mg; Calcium 78mg; Fibre 5.5g; Sodium 8mg.

Mango mania

Even people on a dairy-free diet can enjoy rich, creamy drinks. This one is made using soya milk, which is particularly good in milkshakes and smoothies. It has a lovely caramel flavour that blends brilliantly with fruit purées, especially those made from naturally sweet fruits, like mangoes.

1 Peel the mango and cut the flesh off the pit. Put the chopped flesh in a blender goblet and add the soya milk, lime rind and juice, and a little honey.

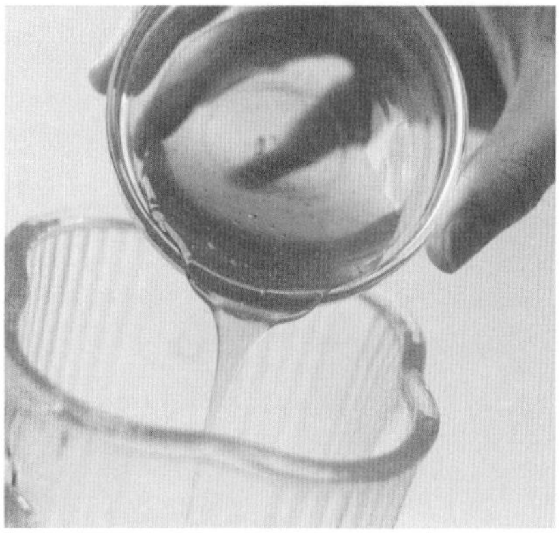

2 Screw on the lid and blitz until smooth and frothy. Taste the mixture and add more honey, if you like, blending well. Place some crushed ice in two glasses, then pour over the smoothie. Sprinkle with lime rind and serve immediately.

Serves 2

1 medium mango

300ml/½ pint/1¼ cups soya milk

finely grated rind and juice of 1 lime, plus extra rind, to decorate

15–30ml/1–2 tbsp clear honey

crushed ice

SMOOTHIE TIP – If you prefer a sweeter taste, choose soya milk sweetened with apple juice for this recipe. It is readily available in supermarkets and has a really rich flavour.

Energy 111kcal/468kJ; Protein 4.9g; Carbohydrate 17.1g, of which sugars 16.9g; Fat 2.6g, of which saturates 0.6g; Cholesterol 0mg; Calcium 29mg; Fibre 2g; Sodium 51mg.

Mango and lime lassi

Serves 2

1 mango

finely grated rind and juice of 1 lime

15ml/1 tbsp lemon juice

5–10ml/1–2 tsp caster/superfine sugar

100ml/3½fl oz/scant ½ cup natural/plain yogurt

mineral water

1 extra lime, halved, to serve

Soft, ripe mango blended with yogurt and sharp, zesty lime and lemon juice makes a wonderfully thick, cooling drink that's packed with energy. Inspired by the classic Indian drink, it can also be enjoyed for breakfast or as a mellow soother when you need to unwind.

1 Peel the mango and cut the flesh from the pit. Put the flesh into a blender goblet with the lime rind and juice. Add the lemon juice, sugar and yogurt. Screw on the lid.

2 Whizz until completely smooth, scraping down from the sides of the goblet if necessary. Stir in a little mineral water to thin it down. Serve immediately, with half a lime on the side of each glass so that more juice can be squeezed in, if desired.

Energy 81kcal/344kJ; Protein 3.1g; Carbohydrate 17g, of which sugars 16.7g; Fat 0.7g, of which saturates 0.4g; Cholesterol 1mg; Calcium 106mg; Fibre 2g; Sodium 43mg.

Apricot squash

Serves 1–2

2 limes

3 oranges

4 ripe apricots

several lemon balm sprigs, plus extra to decorate

SMOOTHIE TIP – This makes a tangy, invigorating blend to wake up your senses. Stir in a little honey or sugar if you find it a bit too tart.

Choose sweet and juicy ripe apricots when they are in season – which can be short. They act as a perfect foil to the tangy limes in this refreshing drink.

1 Squeeze the limes and oranges, either by hand or using a citrus juicer. Halve and pit the apricots.

2 Put the apricots in a blender goblet with a little of the citrus juice and the lemon balm. Screw on the lid and blend until smooth, scraping down from the sides if necessary. Add the remaining juice and blend until smooth.

3 Pour into one medium glass or two short ones and serve decorated with extra lemon balm.

Energy 46kcal/195kJ; Protein 0.9g; Carbohydrate 10.9g, of which sugars 10.9g; Fat 0.2g, of which saturates 0g; Cholesterol 0mg; Calcium 17mg; Fibre 1.1g; Sodium 9mg..

Red defender

Serves 2

200g/7oz/1¾ cups strawberries
90g/3½oz/⅔ cup seedless red grapes
1 small wedge of watermelon

SMOOTHIE TIP - Decorate this smoothie with a chunk of watermelon and/or strawberry halves, if you like.

Boost your body's defences with this delicious blend of red fruits. Watermelon and strawberries are a good source of vitamin C and the black watermelon seeds, like all other seeds, are rich in essential nutrients. If you really don't like the idea of blending the seeds, remove them first.

1 Hull the strawberries and halve them if they are large. Pull the grapes from their stalks. Cut away the skin from the watermelon.

2 Put the watermelon in a blender goblet, screw on the lid and blitz until the seeds are broken up.

3 Add the strawberries and grapes and blend until smooth, scraping down from the sides if necessary. Serve in two glasses.

Energy 85kcal/362kJ; Protein 1.5g; Carbohydrate 20.1g, of which sugars 20.1g; Fat 0.5g, of which saturates 0.1g; Cholesterol 0mg; Calcium 29mg; Fibre 1.5g; Sodium 9mg.

Ruby dreamer

Figs have a distinctive yet delicate taste and are best used in simple combinations, with ingredients that enhance, rather than mask, their flavour. Like most fruits, fresh figs are now available most of the year round but they are often at their best in winter when ruby oranges are also in season – allowing you to make this treat of a smoothie.

1 Cut off the hard, woody tips from the stalks of the figs, then use a sharp knife to cut each fruit in half.

2 Squeeze the oranges and pour the juice into a blender goblet. Add the figs and sugar. Screw on the lid and blitz until smooth, scraping down from the sides of the goblet if necessary.

3 Add lemon juice to taste and blend again. Pour over crushed ice and serve immediately.

Serves 2

6 large ripe figs

4 ruby oranges

15ml/1 tbsp dark muscovado/ molasses sugar

30–45ml/2–3 tbsp lemon juice

crushed ice

SMOOTHIE TIP – If you cannot find ruby oranges, use any other type of orange. The colour of the juice, however, will not be quite so vibrant.

Energy 417kcal/1776kJ; Protein 7.2g; Carbohydrate 97.8g, of which sugars 97.8g; Fat 2.5g, of which saturates 0g; Cholesterol 0mg; Calcium 443mg; Fibre 13.8g; Sodium 96mg.

Rosemary nectar

Serves 3

4 long rosemary sprigs, plus extra to decorate

15ml/1 tbsp golden caster/superfine sugar

2.5ml/½ tsp ground ginger

2 oranges

4 nectarines

ice cubes

SMOOTHIE TIP – If you've bought nectarines only to find that they're as hard as bullets, leave them in the fruit bowl next to some bananas for a couple of days.

This is only worth making if you've got perfectly ripe ingredients. The fabulously aromatic fragrance of fresh rosemary combines with the sweet, scented flavour of juicy nectarines to produce a delicious blend.

1 Put the rosemary sprigs in a pan with the sugar, ginger and 150ml/¼ pint/⅔ cup water. Heat gently until the sugar dissolves, then simmer for 1 minute. Remove from the heat and leave the syrup to steep and cool.

2 Squeeze the oranges. Halve and pit the nectarines and put in a blender goblet with the orange juice. Screw on the lid and process until the mixture is as smooth as possible.

3 Remove the rosemary and pour the syrup into the juice. Blend briefly. Put ice cubes in three glasses and fill with the juice.

Energy 123kcal/527kJ; Protein 3.5g; Carbohydrate 28.7g, of which sugars 28.7g; Fat 0.3g, of which saturates 0g; Cholesterol 0mg; Calcium 61mg; Fibre 3.7g; Sodium 7mg.

Berry blender

Serves 3

500g/1lb 2oz frozen mixed summer fruits, partially thawed

30ml/2 tbsp caster/superfine sugar

about 300ml/½ pint/1¼ cups freshly squeezed orange juice

60ml/4 tbsp cream or yogurt

SMOOTHIE TIP – If you don't want to squeeze the oranges, you can use bought fresh juice instead – but avoid the concentrated type.

Pre-packed and ready to use, a mixed bag of summer fruits (which can be bought from the freezer section in most large supermarkets) makes an unbelievably simple, fruity base for drinks. The frozen fruits mean that the final blend is perfectly chilled as well, so you don't need to add ice. Mixed with orange juice and enriched with a tempting swirl of cream, this smoothie is made in a flash – just the accompaniment to a relaxing afternoon in the sunshine.

1 Tip all but a few of the summer fruits into a blender goblet and add the sugar and orange juice. Screw on the lid and blend until smooth, adding a little more juice if the mixture is too thick.

2 Pour the smoothie into three tall glasses and, using a teaspoon, swirl a little cream or yogurt into each glass. Top with the reserved fruits and serve with long spoons to mix in the cream.

Fruit-tea smoothie

Serves 2

50g/2oz dried apples

25g/1oz dried apricots

2 fruit teabags

juice of 1 lemon

30ml/2 tbsp crème fraîche or natural/plain yogurt

mineral water (optional)

SMOOTHIE TIP – Apple and lemon, apple and mango, forest berries, and strawberry and raspberry fruit teas are just a few of the types you could use.

Depending on your preference you can use any of the varied assortment of fruit teas for this thick, creamy blend. From start to finish, this smoothie takes about one hour to prepare since you need to leave the fruit to steep.

1 Chop the apples and apricots. Steep the teabags in 300ml/½ pint/1¼ cups boiling water for 5 minutes, then remove the teabags.

2 Add the fruit to the tea and leave to stand for 30 minutes. Chill for about 30 minutes until the tea is completely cold.

3 Put the fruit and tea mixture into a blender goblet and add the lemon juice. Screw on the lid and blend well until smooth, scraping down from the sides of the goblet if necessary.

4 Add the crème fraîche or yogurt and blend briefly, adding a little mineral water if the smoothie is too thick. Serve in two glasses.

Berry: Energy 159kcal/669kJ; Protein 2.5g; Carbohydrate 29.7g, of which sugars 29.7g; Fat 4.1g, of which saturates 2.4g; Cholesterol 11mg; Calcium 60mg; Fibre 1.9g; Sodium 26mg
Fruit-tea: Energy 116kcal/486kJ; Protein 1.9g; Carbohydrate 14.1g, of which sugars 14g; Fat 6.2g, of which saturates 4.1g; Cholesterol 17mg; Calcium 36mg; Fibre 2.4g; Sodium 9mg.

Purple haze

Serves 2

250g/9oz/2¼ cups blueberries

50g/2oz/¼ cup caster/superfine sugar

15ml/1 tbsp lemon juice

300ml/½ pint/1¼ cups buttermilk

5ml/1 tsp vanilla extract

150ml/¼ pint/⅔ cup full-fat/whole milk

Thick, dark blueberry purée swirled into pale and creamy vanilla-flavoured buttermilk looks stunning and tastes simply divine. Despite its creaminess, the buttermilk gives this sumptuous smoothie a delicious sharp tang.

1 Push the blueberries through a juicer. Stir in 15ml/1 tbsp of the sugar and the lemon juice. Stir and divide between two glasses.

2 Put the buttermilk, vanilla extract, milk and remaining sugar in a blender goblet, screw on the lid and blitz until really frothy.

3 Pour the buttermilk over the blueberry juice so the mixtures swirl together where they meet – there is no need to stir them together. Serve immediately.

SMOOTHIE TIPS

- Deep violet blueberry juice makes a fantastic contrast in both colour and flavour to the buttermilk. If you can't get hold of blueberries, other slightly tart fruits such as raspberries or blackberries would also work in this creamy combination.
- If you do not like buttermilk or cannot find it in your local supermarket, you could use a mixture of half natural/plain yogurt and half milk instead.

Energy 274kcal/1157kJ; Protein 9.1g; Carbohydrate 54.2g, of which sugars 49.2g; Fat 3.9g, of which saturates 2.4g; Cholesterol 13mg; Calcium 284mg; Fibre 2.5g; Sodium 99mg.

Red blend

Serves 1

25g/1oz/¼ cup dried cranberries

150g/5oz/1¼ cups redcurrants, plus extra to decorate

10ml/2 tsp clear honey

50ml/2fl oz/¼ cup soya milk

sparkling mineral water

SMOOTHIE TIPS

- Allowing sufficient time for the dried cranberries to rehydrate means that they will become plump and juicy, making them easier to blend and maximizing their flavour.
- You could use dried cherries in place of the cranberries, and another dairy or non-dairy milk if you prefer.

Tiny crimson redcurrants make the perfect partner for dried cranberries in this refreshingly tart, sparkling smoothie.

1 Soak the cranberries in a bowl with 90ml/6 tbsp boiling water for 10 minutes. String the redcurrants by drawing the stems through the tines of a fork to pull off the delicate currants.

2 Put the currants in a blender goblet along with the cranberries and soaking water. Screw on the lid and blend well until smooth, then add the honey and milk and whizz briefly to combine.

3 Pour the shake into a large glass, then top with a little sparkling mineral water. Decorate with redcurrants and serve immediately.

Energy 126kcal/539kJ; Protein 3.8g; Carbohydrate 27.1g, of which sugars 27.1g; Fat 1g, of which saturates 0.1g; Cholesterol 0mg; Calcium 115mg; Fibre 7g; Sodium 25mg.

Berry vanilla smoother

This simple recipe uses oat milk, a cholesterol-free, calcium-rich alternative to cow's milk, and a good partner to sweet summer fruits. For a really chilled, extremely refreshing flavour, use a mixed bag of semi-thawed frozen fruits, which will blend to a fabulously thick consistency.

Serves 2

250g/9oz frozen mixed summer fruits, partially thawed, plus extra to decorate

130g/4½oz/generous ½ cup soya yogurt

45ml/3 tbsp vanilla syrup

350ml/12fl oz/1½ cups oat milk

1 Put the summer fruits in a blender goblet. Add the yogurt, screw on the lid and blend to make a purée. Scrape the mixture down from the sides of the goblet if necessary, then blend again.

2 Add the vanilla syrup and oat milk to the fruit purée and blend the mixture again until smooth.

3 Transfer the smoothie to a small jug or pitcher and chill, or pour it into two tall glasses and serve immediately, decorated with the extra fruits.

SMOOTHIE TIP – Vanilla syrup is sweet and full of flavour, making it great for giving drinks and desserts a deep, mellow taste.

Pear, rhubarb and cranberry cooler

For best results, use really ripe pears. Do not forget to cook the rhubarb well in advance so that it has plenty of time to cool down before you start blending.

Serves 3–4

400g/14oz early rhubarb

2 large ripe pears

130g/4½oz/generous 1 cup fresh or frozen cranberries

90g/3½oz/½ cup caster/superfine sugar

mineral water (optional)

1 Trim the rhubarb and cut into 2cm/¾in lengths. Place in a pan with 90ml/6 tbsp water and cover with a tight-fitting lid. Cook gently for about 5 minutes or until tender. Transfer to a bowl and leave to cool, putting several pieces aside for a decoration.

2 Peel, quarter and core the pears and tip into a blender goblet with the cranberries, the rhubarb and its juices, and the sugar.

3 Screw on the lid and blend until smooth, scraping down from the sides if necessary. Thin with mineral water, if liked. Serve, decorated with the rhubarb pieces.

Berry: Energy 204kcal/856kJ; Protein 9.4g; Carbohydrate 29.2g, of which sugars 29.2g; Fat 4.1g, of which saturates 0.9g; Cholesterol 1mg; Calcium 47mg; Fibre 1.4g; Sodium 125mg.
Pear: Energy 138kcal/590kJ; Protein 1.4g; Carbohydrate 34.9g, of which sugars 34.9g; Fat 0.2g, of which saturates 0g; Cholesterol 0mg; Calcium 115mg; Fibre 3.6g; Sodium 7mg.

Pink 'gin'

Serves 4

600g/1lb 6oz rhubarb

finely grated rind and juice of 2 limes

75g/3oz/6 tbsp caster/superfine sugar

15ml/1 tbsp juniper berries, lightly crushed

ice cubes

lime slices, quartered

sparkling mineral water, soda water/club soda or real lemonade

Juniper berries are a vital ingredient in the making of gin and, not surprisingly, they exude distinct gin-like aromas in this fabulous non-alcoholic drink. For a good colour, this is best made using early, forced rhubarb, which gives the juice a characteristic pink blush. Top up the 'gin' with some chilled sparkling water, or use real lemonade for a delicious, tangy taste. You could also add a shot of actual gin for a boozy version.

1 Using a sharp knife, chop the rhubarb into 2cm/¾in lengths and place in a pan with the lime rind and juice.

2 Add the sugar, crushed juniper berries and 90ml/6 tbsp water. Cover with a tight-fitting lid and cook for 6–8 minutes, until the rhubarb is just tender. Test by prodding the rhubarb with the tip of a knife.

3 Transfer the rhubarb to a blender goblet, screw on the lid and process to form a smooth purée. Press the mixture through a coarse sieve or strainer into a bowl and set the strained liquid aside until completely cold.

4 Half-fill four medium glasses with the rhubarb purée. Add ice cubes and lime slices and top up with sparkling mineral water, soda water or lemonade. Serve immediately.

SMOOTHIE TIPS

- If the rhubarb syrup is stored for a couple of days in the fridge after straining, the juniper flavour will become a little bit more pronounced.
- The overall intensity is better if the drink is made with just rhubarb, but you could use a mixture of apple and rhubarb, if you prefer.

Energy 50kcal/207kJ; Protein 0g; Carbohydrate 0g, of which sugars 0g; Fat 0g, of which saturates 0g; Cholesterol 0mg; Calcium 0mg; Fibre 0g; Sodium 0mg.

Raspberry and oatmeal

Serves 1

25ml/1½ tbsp medium oatmeal

150g/5oz/scant 1 cup raspberries, plus a couple to decorate

5–10ml/1–2 tsp clear honey

45ml/3 tbsp natural/plain yogurt

SMOOTHIE TIP – For a smooth finish, press the fruit through a sieve or strainer before serving.

Just a spoonful or so of oatmeal gives substance to this invigorating drink. If you can, prepare it ahead of time because soaking the raw oats helps to break down the starch into natural sugars that are easy to digest.

1 Soak the oatmeal in 120ml/4fl oz/½ cup boiling water for 10 minutes. Transfer to a blender goblet and add the raspberries, honey and 30ml/2 tbsp of the yogurt. Screw on the lid and blitz until smooth, scraping down from the sides if necessary.

2 Pour into a large glass, swirl in the remaining yogurt and top with the reserved raspberries.

Energy 186kcal/793kJ; Protein 7.5g; Carbohydrate 34.6g, of which sugars 16.4g; Fat 3.1g, of which saturates 0.4g; Cholesterol 1mg; Calcium 137mg; Fibre 5.4g; Sodium 51mg.

Peach, banana and raspberry

Whizzed up in just minutes, this thick, slightly tart smoothie makes a good stop-gap between meals, a brilliant easy-to-eat breakfast, or even a healthy – and tasty – dessert.

1 Halve, pit and chop the peach, break the banana into pieces and put both in a blender goblet. Screw on the lid and blend until smooth, scraping the mixture down from the sides if necessary.

2 Add the raspberries and blend until smooth. Pour into two glasses and top up with mineral water, if using. Add ice cubes, decorate with extra raspberries and serve with straws or spoons.

Serves 2

1 large ripe peach

1 small banana, peeled

130g/4½oz/¾ cup fresh or frozen raspberries, plus extra to decorate

still or sparkling mineral water (optional)

ice cubes

Energy 66kcal/282kJ; Protein 1.8g; Carbohydrate 15g, of which sugars 14g; Fat 0.4g, of which saturates 0.1g; Cholesterol 0mg; Calcium 21mg; Fibre 2.6g; Sodium 3mg.

Raspberry and apple blend

Although usually put through the juicer for drinking, apples can be blended as long as you process them well. This recipe is thinned with fresh apple juice.

Serves 2

- 2 eating apples
- 10ml/2 tsp caster/superfine sugar
- 15ml/1 tbsp lemon juice
- 130g/4½oz/¾ cup fresh or frozen raspberries
- 150ml/¼ pint/⅔ cup apple juice
- 15–30ml/1–2 tbsp rose water
- whole raspberries and rose petals, to decorate (optional)

1 Peel and core the apples and put them in a blender goblet with the sugar and lemon juice. Blend well until smooth, scraping down from the sides if necessary.

2 Add the raspberries and apple juice to the apple purée, screw on the lid and blend until completely smooth. Add the rose water and blend briefly to combine.

3 Pour the smoothie into two medium glasses and place whole raspberries and rose petals on top, to decorate, if you like. Serve immediately, or chill in the fridge until ready to serve.

Coconut, banana and hazelnut

This nutty, rich and creamy drink is one to sip at your leisure. Leftovers can be put in the fridge for up to a couple of days, in which time the flavour of the hazelnuts will develop.

Serves 2

- 90g/3½oz/scant 1 cup whole blanched hazelnuts
- 1 banana, sliced
- 30ml/2 tbsp golden caster/superfine sugar
- 2.5ml/½ tsp almond extract
- 200ml/7fl oz/scant 1 cup coconut cream
- 30ml/2 tbsp double/heavy cream (optional)
- 150ml/¼ pint/⅔ cup mineral water
- crushed ice

1 Chop the hazelnuts and lightly toast them in a small frying pan, turning frequently. Leave to cool, then tip into a blender goblet with the sugar and blend until very finely ground. Add the banana, almond extract, coconut cream and double cream, if using. Screw on the lid and blend thoroughly until smooth.

2 Strain the mixture through a sieve or strainer into a jug or pitcher, pressing the pulp down with the back of a spoon to extract as much liquid as possible. Stir in the mineral water.

3 Half-fill two glasses with crushed ice and pour over the nut smoothie. Serve the drinks immediately, or chill in the fridge until ready to serve.

Raspberry: Energy 91kcal/391kJ; Protein 1.3g; Carbohydrate 22.3g, of which sugars 22.3g; Fat 0.4g, of which saturates 0.1g; Cholesterol 0mg; Calcium 27mg; Fibre 2.9g; Sodium 6mg.
Coconut: Energy 364kcal/1514kJ; Protein 6.7g; Carbohydrate 20.7g, of which sugars 19.8g; Fat 28.9g, of which saturates 2.3g; Cholesterol 0mg; Calcium 99mg; Fibre 2.9g; Sodium 114mg.

Tutti-frutti with ice pops

Serves 2

1 apple

300ml/½ pint/1¼ cups apple juice

2 kiwi fruit

90g/3½oz/generous ½ cup raspberries

10ml/2 tsp caster/superfine sugar

150g/5oz/1 cup seedless red grapes

150g/5oz/1¼ cups blackcurrants or blackberries

1 large banana, peeled and sliced

Chunky ice-lolly stirrers accompany this fruit-packed smoothie giving it plenty of child-appeal, great for an after-school treat on a hot day. The lollies can be frozen ahead and stored so they're ready on demand, and the juice takes just moments to prepare.

1 To make the ice pops, peel, core and roughly chop the apple. Place in a blender goblet with 100ml/3½fl oz/scant ½ cup of the apple juice, screw on the lid and blend to a smooth purée. Pour into a third of the sections of an ice-cube tray.

2 Peel and roughly chop the kiwi fruit, screw on the lid and blend until smooth with 100ml/3½fl oz/scant ½ cup of the apple juice. Pour into another third of the ice-cube tray sections.

3 Blend the raspberries with the sugar and the remaining apple juice in the blender goblet and spoon into the final sections.

4 Freeze the tray for about 30 minutes, then push a wooden ice-lolly or popsicle stick into each. Freeze until solid.

5 To make the smoothie, put the grapes, blackcurrants or blackberries, and banana into the blender goblet, screw on the lid and blend until smooth. If you like, push the mixture through a coarse sieve or strainer after blending to remove the seeds and skins.

6 To serve, push fruit lollies out of the tray and place them on serving plates. Pour the fruit smoothie into two glasses and place on the plates with the lollies.

7 Serve immediately as the lollies will start to melt very quickly – and don't forget to supply plenty of napkins!

Energy 231kcal/986kJ; Protein 3g; Carbohydrate 56.2g, of which sugars 55.1g; Fat 1g, of which saturates 0.1g; Cholesterol 0mg; Calcium 84mg; Fibre 6.1g; Sodium 11mg.

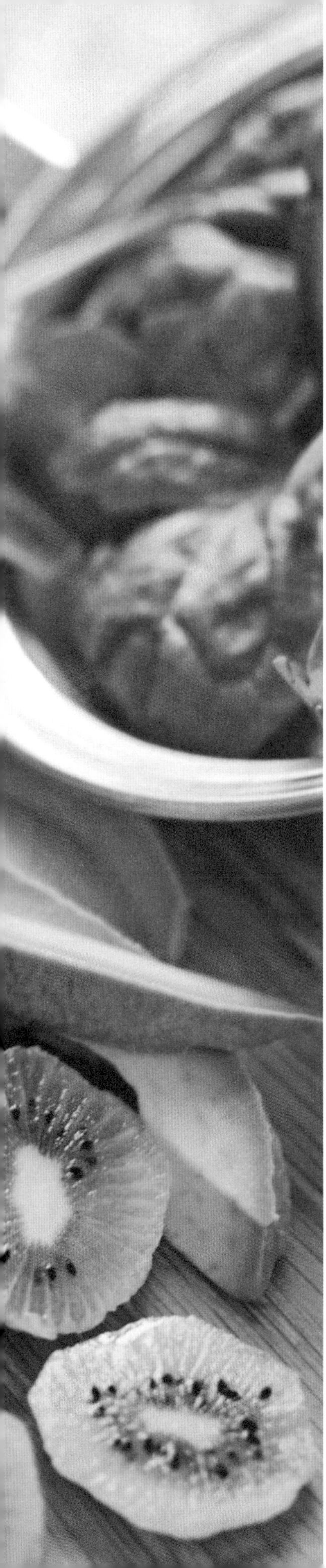

Green smoothies

We all need an energy boost at some point during the day, perhaps before or after an exercise class or run, to keep you on top form in a pressurized job, or to cope with the stresses and strains of everyday life. Made with avocados, bananas, papaya, nuts and seeds, these drinks are higher in energy-boosting carbs and calories than some of the green juices, but also provide all-important slow-release energy to fight fatigue and maintain concentration levels.

Digestive soother

Serves 1

150ml/¼ pint/⅔ cup barley water

1 thin slice of fresh root ginger, no need to peel

50g/2oz or 2 cauliflower florets

75g/3oz/½ cup seedless green grapes

1 small banana, sliced

4 outer romaine lettuce leaves

fresh lime juice (optional)

Our digestive system breaks down the food we eat into easily absorbed nutrients to build and maintain cells in our body, but the process is only as good as the foods that we put in. Just like a car, add the wrong kind of fuel and the engine won't perform as well. If you have over-indulged and are suffering with indigestion, try this gingered barley and banana smoothie to settle your stomach.

1 Put the barley water in a blender goblet along with the ginger, cauliflower and grapes. Add the banana and lettuce, then screw on the lid and blitz until smooth.

2 Pour into a glass and add lime juice to taste, if liked.

Energy 177kcal/753kJ; Protein 3.8g; Carbohydrate 40.7g, of which sugars 38.7g; Fat 1.1g, of which saturates 0.2g; Cholesterol 0mg; Calcium 40mg; Fibre 4g; Sodium 12mg.

Heartburn healer

If you have overdone it a little with too much rich food or a glass or two of wine more than you should have had, this soothing yogurt-based smoothie may help to relieve symptoms of heartburn or acid reflux. Papaya contains the enzyme papain, which is used in many acid reflux medicines.

1 Put all the ingredients in a blender goblet, screw on the lid and blitz until smooth.

2 Adjust the consistency of the smoothie by adding a little extra water, if you like.

3 Pour into two glasses, sprinkle with some extra chopped almonds and serve immediately.

Serves 2

- 125ml/4fl oz/½ cup natural/plain low-fat or non-dairy yogurt
- ½ banana, peeled and sliced
- ½ papaya, seeded, no need to peel, cut into chunks
- 25g/1oz or 1 cauliflower floret
- 25g/1oz/1 cup baby spinach leaves
- 10 unblanched almonds, plus a few extra chopped, to decorate
- 125ml/4fl oz/½ cup water

Energy 322kcal/1363kJ; Protein 11.9g; Carbohydrate 54.6g, of which sugars 52.5g; Fat 7.7g, of which saturates 1.4g; Cholesterol 2mg; Calcium 340mg; Fibre 11.2g; Sodium 130mg.

Triple nut combo

Serves 1

250ml/8fl oz/1 cup unsweetened almond milk

25g/1oz/¼ cup Brazil nuts

25g/1oz/¼ cup hazelnuts

25g/1oz/1 cup baby spinach leaves

1 small banana, peeled and sliced

a few drops of vanilla extract

a little water or ice cubes, to taste

All the taste and creamy smoothness of a dairy shake, yet this is made with nuts and nut milk for a high-energy, protein- and vitamin E-packed drink. The spinach has such a delicate flavour that if it weren't for the colour you would have no idea that a green vegetable had been added.

1 Put all the ingredients in a blender goblet with the exception of the water. Screw on the lid and blitz until really smooth.

2 Add a little water or handful of ice cubes and blitz again until it has the desired thickness. Pour into a tall glass to serve.

SMOOTHIE TIP – If you're using fresh cut spinach from the garden or a farm store, make sure that you rinse off all traces of soil before using it.

NUTRIENT NOTE – Nuts are packed with protein, an essential part of every cell in our body and needed for growth and repair of everything from muscles and bones to hair and fingernails. Protein also aids digestion, produces antibodies that fight off infection and boosts hormones so that our body works efficiently. Nuts do contain fat but it is the healthy unsaturated fatty acids rather than the saturated fat found in red meat.

Energy 448kcal/1857kJ; Protein 9.7g; Carbohydrate 24.1g, of which sugars 21.8g; Fat 35.4g, of which saturates 5.6g; Cholesterol 0mg; Calcium 124mg; Fibre 5.3g; Sodium 205mg.

Totally tropical

A mild, soothing smoothie with just a hint of ginger, this healthy drink is packed with fibre and natural fruit sugars to kickstart the day and provide slow-release energy to help avoid mood swings and aid concentration at work.

Serves 1

¼ medium pineapple, peeled, core left in, cut into chunks

½ small mango, pitted, peeled and cut into chunks

25g/1oz/1 cup shredded kale

50g/2oz/½ cup broccoli florets, quartered

1cm/½in piece of fresh root ginger, no need to peel, halved

125ml/4fl oz/½ cup canned light coconut milk

175ml/6fl oz/¾ cup water

1 Put all the fruit and vegetables in a blender goblet. Add the ginger then pour in the coconut milk and water. Screw on the lid and blitz until smooth.

2 Pour into a tall glass and serve.

SMOOTHIE TIP – If your blender goblet is small then add just half the water, blitz until smooth, then adjust to the desired thickness with the remaining water.

NUTRIENT NOTE – Kale is rich in fibre, which is essential to aid digestion and to help lower cholesterol. The Department of Health suggests we should all be eating at least 40 per cent more fibre or 5g a day more to take us up to the recommended 18g a day. Although fibre is not digested it nourishes the bacteria in the large bowel and slows the absorption of glucose in the small intestine, so that energy is released gradually and avoids the sugar highs and lows that cause mood swings.

Energy 177kcal/758kJ; Protein 4.8g; Carbohydrate 38.1g, of which sugars 37.8g; Fat 1.8g, of which saturates 0.5g; Cholesterol 0mg; Calcium 142mg; Fibre 8.6g; Sodium 158mg.

Green tornado

Serves 1

15g/½oz/½ cup shredded kale

25g/1oz/1 cup baby spinach leaves

100g/3¾oz/generous ⅔ cup seedless green grapes

½ ripe ripe avocado, pitted, flesh scooped from the skin

250ml/8fl oz/1 cup coconut water from a carton

a few ice cubes

juice of ½ lime

SMOOTHIE TIP – Having a ripe avocado is essential for this smoothie. If it is under-ripe you won't be able to get a really smooth texture.

Bursting with complex carbs and natural fruit sugars, this velvety nutrient-bursting tornado of a smoothie will superpower you through any sporting activity or boost energy levels post exercise.

1 Put the kale, spinach, grapes and avocado in a blender goblet then pour in the coconut water. Screw on the lid and blitz until smooth. Add the ice cubes and blitz again until crushed.

2 Pour into a glass and add lime juice to taste. Serve immediately.

Energy 261kcal/1088kJ; Protein 3.5g; Carbohydrate 17.9g, of which sugars 16.5g; Fat 20g, of which saturates 4.2g; Cholesterol 0mg; Calcium 86mg; Fibre 6.8g; Sodium 49mg.

Green giant

Serves 1

1 kiwi fruit, peeled and cut into chunks

½ small ripe avocado, pitted, flesh scooped from the skin

15g/½oz/½ cup baby spinach leaves

15g/½oz/½ cup shredded kale

10ml/2 tsp unflavoured pea protein powder

2.5ml/½ tsp camu camu powder

250ml/8fl oz/1 cup coconut water from a carton, or water

This thick, filling and sustaining smoothie really is a meal in a glass and a much healthier option than a caffeine- and calorie-laden cappuccino-style coffee.

1 Put the kiwi fruit, avocado, spinach and kale leaves in a blender goblet. Spoon in the protein powder and camu camu powder, then pour in the coconut water.

2 Screw on the lid and blitz until really smooth. If your blender goblet is small then add just half the coconut water and blitz together until smooth, then add the remaining coconut water and blitz until smooth once more.

3 Pour into a tall glass and serve immediately.

SMOOTHIE TIP – If you are new to green smoothies you may like to add a little honey or maple syrup. As you get a taste for green juices and eat less processed food you will also find that you crave less sweet food and may not want to add any extra sweetness at all.

NUTRIENT NOTE – Camu camu powder is made from a sour red berry and is packed with vitamin C and antioxidants, among other things. Due to its tart taste, take care not to add too much or it will affect the flavour of your shake.

Energy 216kcal/899kJ; Protein 11.2g; Carbohydrate 8.6g, of which sugars 7g; Fat 15.5g, of which saturates 3.1g; Cholesterol 0mg; Calcium 68mg; Fibre 6.3g; Sodium 34mg.

Immune booster

The immune system is essential in protecting our health; each illness, injury or threat to our body stimulates a response for the body to heal itself. Vitamin C is crucial to maintaining and boosting immune levels, and as it can't be stored by the body it is needed on a daily basis. This tasty and refreshing drink keeps us on track.

Serves 1

15g/½oz/½ cup shredded kale

15g/½oz/½ cup baby spinach leaves

10g/¼oz/½ cup parsley

1 kiwi fruit, peeled and cut into chunks

½ pear, cored, skin left on, cut into chunks

50g/2oz/2 strawberries, hulled

15ml/1 tbsp ground seed mix, see p115

125ml/4fl oz/½ cup water

1 Put all the ingredients in a blender goblet, screw on the lid and blitz together until smooth.

2 Pour into a tall glass to serve.

SMOOTHIE TIP - Mixed seeds are a great way to boost protein, vitamin and mineral levels. So that the body can absorb as much of their nutritional value as possible, grind them before eating or drinking them. For ease, packs of ready-ground flaxseeds are sold in the supermarket and could also be used in place of the homemade ground seed mix.

Energy 295kcal/1233kJ; Protein 8.8g; Carbohydrate 44.6g, of which sugars 44.3g; Fat 10g, of which saturates 1.6g; Cholesterol 0mg; Calcium 266mg; Fibre 14g; Sodium 79mg.

Summer herb sensation

Packed with light flavours, fresh herbs are antibacterial, anti-inflammatory, rich in antioxidants, and taste delicious mixed with refreshing melon and tangy kiwi fruit.

1 Put all the ingredients in a blender goblet except the lime juice. Screw on the lid and blitz until smooth.

2 Pour into a tall glass and stir in lime juice to taste.

Serves 1

2 fresh parsley stems

2 fresh mint stems

2 fresh basil stems

225g/8oz or ¼ green-fleshed melon, seeded, peeled and cut into chunks

1 kiwi fruit, peeled and cut into chunks

250ml/8fl oz/1 cup water

squeeze of fresh lime, to taste

SMOOTHIE TIP – Transplant pots of supermarket herbs into larger pots at home and keep them on the windowsill or by the back door; water them regularly and they will continue to grow for several months.

Energy 70kcal/298kJ; Protein 1.9g; Carbohydrate 15.2g, of which sugars 14.9g; Fat 0.6g, of which saturates 0g; Cholesterol 0mg; Calcium 64mg; Fibre 3.3g; Sodium 54mg.

Spring clean

Serves 1

¼ small fennel bulb or ¼ cup when roughly chopped

25g/1oz/1 cup baby spinach leaves

50g/2oz or 2 cauliflower florets

½ pear, no need to peel or core, cut into chunks

75g/3oz/½ cup seedless green grapes

250ml/8fl oz/1 cup water

NUTRIENT NOTE – Herbalists have long thought of fennel as a help with digestion problems including heartburn, intestinal gas, bloating and loss of appetite. This Mediterranean vegetable has a delicate, slightly sweet anise-like flavour.

While we all know we should eat at least five portions of fruit and veg a day it is easy to get into bad habits. Get back on track with this mild green juice – the gentle way to soothe and cleanse the digestive system.

1 Put all the ingredients in a blender goblet, screw on the lid and blitz until smooth.

2 Pour into a tall glass to serve.

Energy 96kcal/407kJ; Protein 2.8g; Carbohydrate 20.8g, of which sugars 20.6g; Fat 0.7g, of which saturates 0.1g; Cholesterol 0mg; Calcium 71mg; Fibre 0.8g; Sodium 43mg.

Kiwi reviver

Serves 1

1 kiwi fruit, peeled and roughly chopped

¼ medium pineapple, peeled, core left in, roughly chopped

25g/1oz/1 cup baby spinach leaves

5cm/2in piece of cucumber, diced

125ml/4fl oz/½ cup water

5ml/1 tsp chia seeds

SMOOTHIE TIP – Chia seeds swell when they come into contact with liquid so drink this as soon as you have made it or you may find you will need a spoon! Once drunk, the gelling action in your stomach will give the sensation of feeling fuller for longer.

This eye-catching, bright-green, tangy smoothie is speckled with tiny black chia seeds, which are a powerhouse of nutrition – rich in soluble fibre, minerals and omega 3 fatty acids, and beneficial for brain function, cardiovascular health, and lowering inflammation.

1 Put all the ingredients except the chia seeds in a blender goblet, screw on the lid and blitz until smooth.

2 Stir in the chia seeds and a little extra water, if needed. Pour into a tall glass and serve immediately.

Energy 190kcal/796kJ; Protein 7.5g; Carbohydrate 35.7g, of which sugars 29.3g; Fat 2.7g, of which saturates 0.5g; Cholesterol 0mg; Calcium 204mg; Fibre 1.7g; Sodium 84mg.

Papaya passion

Just half a papaya provides an adult's daily allowance of vitamin C, which is not only needed to boost immunity but also to produce collagen vital for muscle strength, healthy skin and bones, and to stimulate production of white blood cells to help fight infection. Its creamy delicate-tasting flesh adds a wonderful velvety smoothness to this shake.

1 Put all the ingredients in a blender goblet, screw on the lid and blitz until smooth.

2 Pour into a tall glass and serve.

SMOOTHIE TIP – If pea shoots are out of season you can instead add 25g/1oz/1 cup baby spinach leaves or a mixture of spinach and lettuce leaves.

Serves 1

½ papaya, seeds discarded, peeled, flesh cut into chunks

2 passion fruits, halved, pulp and seeds scooped out

15g/½oz/¾ cup pea shoots

30ml/2 tbsp desiccated/dry unsweetened shredded coconut

125ml/4fl oz/½ cup natural/plain low-fat or non-dairy yogurt

125ml/4fl oz/½ cup coconut water from a carton

Energy 414kcal/1738kJ; Protein 10.7g; Carbohydrate 49.9g, of which sugars 49.8g; Fat 20.5g, of which saturates 16.9g; Cholesterol 2mg; Calcium 327mg; Fibre 19.5g; Sodium 132mg.

First defence

Fight those winter cold and flu bugs with this foodie fusion, which consists of old-fashioned lemon barley water blended with a more modern green spinach-based smoothie.

Serves 1–2

100g/3¾oz/½ cup pearl/pot barley

600ml/1 pint/2½ cups water

1 orange, rind and pith cut away, cut into chunks

½ lemon, rind and pith cut away, cut into chunks

1 small slice of fresh root ginger, no need to peel, quartered

25g/1oz/1 cup baby spinach leaves

5ml/1 tsp honey or sweetener of choice

1 Put the pearl barley and water in a pan, bring to the boil, then cover the pan and simmer gently for 30 minutes.

2 Drain the barley through a sieve or strainer and collect the liquid in a measuring jug or cup. You should have about 300ml/½ pint/ 1¼ cups of barley water.

3 Add 150ml/¼ pint/⅔ cup of the warm barley water and 30ml/ 2 tbsp of the barley to a blender goblet, then add the orange, lemon, ginger and spinach. Screw on the lid and blitz until the mixture is completely smooth.

4 Pour into one or two glasses and stir in honey or sweetener of choice, to taste. Serve warm.

SMOOTHIE TIP - Keep back another 30ml/2 tbsp of cooked barley and the remaining barley water so that you can make this drink again. The remaining cooked barley makes a great high-fibre salad base: mix it with chopped fresh herbs, diced tomato, shredded kale, grated carrot and perhaps a little crumbled feta cheese, all tossed in a lemony vinaigrette dressing.

Energy 112kcal/474kJ; Protein 3.3g; Carbohydrate 24.9g, of which sugars 24.9g; Fat 0.6g, of which saturates 0.1g; Cholesterol 0mg; Calcium 187mg; Fibre 3.4g; Sodium 55mg.

Healthy heart

Serves 1

25g/1oz/1 cup shredded kale
25g/1oz or 6 sugar snap peas
1 banana, peeled and sliced
½ pear, quartered, cored but not peeled, cut into chunks
30ml/2 tbsp rolled oats
250ml/8fl oz/1 cup unsweetened oat milk
1.5ml/¼ tsp spirulina powder (optional)

NUTRIENT NOTE – High-fibre oats and naturally occurring pectin in pears (and apples) have been shown to help lower harmful cholesterol and to help regulate blood pressure.

The World Health Organization says that more people die annually from cardiovascular disease than from any other cause. By making small dietary changes, such as introducing a daily juice or shake, and maintaining them, you can really make a difference to your long-term health.

1 Put all the ingredients except the spirulina in a blender goblet, screw on the lid and blitz until smooth with a few green speckles.

2 Pour into a tall glass, sprinkle with spirulina if using, mix with a fork, then serve.

Energy 400kcal/1686kJ; Protein 7.3g; Carbohydrate 56.6g, of which sugars 39.7g; Fat 6.4g, of which saturates 0.2g; Cholesterol 0mg; Calcium 77mg; Fibre 7.9g; Sodium 25mg.

Minted melon crush

This smooth operator is refreshingly cool on a hot day and will quickly rehydrate you, at the same time as boosting vitamin and mineral levels. Forget about Moroccan mint tea; this low-sugar version is much healthier.

1 Put all the ingredients in a blender goblet, screw on the lid and blitz until smooth.

2 Pour into a tall glass over ice cubes to serve.

Serves 1–3

200g/7oz or ¼ green-fleshed melon, seeded, peeled, flesh cut into chunks

1 kiwi fruit, peeled and roughly chopped

6 mint leaves

25g/1oz/1 cup baby spinach leaves

225ml/8fl oz/1 cup coconut water from a carton

juice of ½ lime

5ml/1 tsp lacuma powder

ice cubes

NUTRIENT NOTE – Lacuma is a fruit found growing in Peru. It is often sold in powdered form in the health food store, and is a natural sweetener.

Energy 90kcal/379kJ; Protein 2.7g; Carbohydrate 19.1g, of which sugars 18.9g; Fat 0.7g, of which saturates 0g; Cholesterol 0mg; Calcium 89mg; Fibre 4.3g; Sodium 91mg.

Stamina maximizer

Serves 1

½ ripe avocado, pitted, flesh scooped from the skin

½ small papaya, seeds discarded, peeled and cut into chunks

25g/1oz/1 cup baby spinach leaves

10 unblanched almonds

10ml/2 tsp ground seed mix, see p115, or ground flaxseeds

250ml/8fl oz/1 cup unsweetened almond milk

125ml/4fl oz/½ cup water

juice of ½ lime

5ml/1 tsp honey (optional)

Thick, creamy and super-satisfying, this pale-green avocado and papaya shake will provide slowly-released energy to power you through any sporting activity, or help boost concentration levels and keep you on target if you are stuck at your desk. It also makes an excellent breakfast.

1 Put the avocado and papaya in a blender goblet, then add the spinach, nuts and seeds. Pour in the almond milk, screw on the lid and blitz until smooth.

2 Adjust the consistency to taste with water, then stir in lime juice and honey to taste, if using. Pour into a glass and serve.

SMOOTHIE TIP – Unsweetened almond milk has been used here but you could substitute rice milk or oat milk or simply add water, if preferred.

NUTRIENT NOTE – Even at rest, our brain uses 50 per cent of the energy that is derived from the food that we consume, and considerably more when we engage our brain when working or sitting an exam or doing a sporting activity. During periods of stress we use up even more energy. We get energy from carbohydrates, protein and fat, all of which can be found in this smooth blend.

Energy 457kcal/1904kJ; Protein 13.1g; Carbohydrate 32.3g, of which sugars 31g; Fat 31.6g, of which saturates 3g; Cholesterol 0mg; Calcium 252mg; Fibre 7.8g; Sodium 220mg.

Cacao and avocado smoothie

A rich chocolatey hit with a velvety texture, this smoothie will leave you feeling re-energized and raring to go.

1 Put all the ingredients in a blender goblet, screw on the lid and blitz until smooth.

2 Pour into a tall glass and serve.

Serves 1

10ml/2 tsp raw cacao powder

10ml/2 tsp dried goji berries

15ml/1 tbsp ground seed mix, see p115

½ ripe avocado, pitted, flesh scooped from the skin

½ small banana, peeled and sliced

½ orange, freshly squeezed juice and flesh scraped from the shell

25g/1oz/1 cup shredded kale

125ml/4fl oz/½ cup canned light coconut milk

125ml/4fl oz/½ cup water

SMOOTHIE TIP - Oranges that have been kept at room temperature are not only easier to squeeze, but you will also get more juice out of them.

NUTRIENT NOTE - Avocados and coconut milk do contain fat, but they are good fats. While we should watch the kinds of fat that we eat, we still need fat for every cell in our body; it insulates us from heat loss, cushions vital organs and provides essential fatty acids as well as aiding the absorption of fat-soluble vitamins. Weight-for-weight, fat provides about three times as much energy as carbohydrates.

Energy 556kcal/1778kJ; Protein 10.1g; Carbohydrate 33.9g, of which sugars 27.2g; Fat 31.7g, of which saturates 7.9g; Cholesterol 0mg; Calcium 224mg; Fibre 11.1g; Sodium 253mg.

Cacao cup

Serves 1

½ banana, peeled and sliced

½ pear, cored, leave skin on, cut into chunks

25g/1oz/1 cup baby spinach leaves

10ml/2 tsp raw cacao powder

10ml/2 tsp ground golden flaxseeds

10ml/2 tsp pea protein or hemp powder

5ml/1 tsp chia seeds

250ml/8fl oz/1 cup unsweetened almond milk

NUTRIENT NOTE – Flaxseeds are super-rich in omega 3 fatty acids and fibre, and are one of the richest sources of plant lignans, which are antioxidants and phytoestrogens. They are gluten free and cholesterol free. Always grind the seeds before adding them to a shake so that the body can absorb as much of the nutritional content as possible during digestion. It also isn't especially pleasant to drink the whole seeds, which are larger than chia seeds.

When dieting, you often long for that chocolate fix. This comforting, creamy-tasting smoothie is dairy free and flavoured with a little raw cacao powder and vanilla for an intense taste that's rich in protein and lower in calories than your usual dairy chocolate drink.

1 Put all the ingredients in a blender goblet, screw on the lid and blitz until smooth.

2 Pour into a cup or glass and serve sprinkled with a few extra chia seeds if liked.

Energy 250kcal/1054kJ; Protein 21.8g; Carbohydrate 26.7g, of which sugars 23.6g; Fat 6.8g, of which saturates 1.6g; Cholesterol 0mg; Calcium 92mg; Fibre 8.4g; Sodium 349mg.

Green devil

Choose a well-flavoured avocado, such as a knobbly, dark-skinned Haas, for this slightly spicy, hot and sour smoothie. Cucumber adds a refreshing edge, while lemon and lime juice zip up the flavour, and the chilli sauce adds an irresistible fiery bite. This is one little devil that is sure to liven up even the most lethargic of days.

Serves 2–3

1 small ripe avocado

½ cucumber

30ml/2 tbsp lemon juice

30ml/2 tbsp lime juice

10ml/2 tsp caster/superfine sugar

a pinch of salt

250ml/8fl oz/1 cup apple juice or mineral water

10–20ml/2–4 tsp sweet chilli sauce

ice cubes

fresh red chilli curls (see Smoothie Tip), to decorate (optional)

1 Halve the avocado and use a sharp knife to remove the pit. Scoop the flesh from both halves into a blender goblet.

2 Peel and roughly chop the cucumber and add to the blender goblet, then add the lemon and lime juice, the sugar and a pinch of salt.

3 Screw on the lid, then process the ingredients until smooth and creamy. Add the apple juice or mineral water and a little of the chilli sauce. Blend briefly once more to combine the ingredients together.

4 Pour the smoothie over ice cubes in two or three glasses. Decorate with red chilli curls, if using, and serve.

SMOOTHIE TIP – To make chilli curls, core and seed a fresh red chilli and cut it into very fine strips. Put the strips in a bowl of iced water and leave to stand for 20 minutes or until the strips curl. Use them to decorate this smoothie.

NUTRIENT NOTE – Seductively smooth avocados are as good for you as they taste. Their fresh vitamin- and mineral-rich flesh is reputed to be fantastic for healthy hair and skin.

Energy 143kcal/598kJ; Protein 1.3g; Carbohydrate 13.2g, of which sugars 12.5g; Fat 9.8g, of which saturates 2.1g; Cholesterol 0mg; Calcium 19mg; Fibre 1.9g; Sodium 6mg.

Hormone balance – women

Serves 1

1 passion fruit, halved

1 small banana, peeled and sliced

40g/1½oz or 3 small broccoli florets

15g/½oz/½ cup shredded kale leaves

15ml/1 tbsp ground seed mix, see p115

15ml/1 tbsp dried goji berries, plus a few extra to decorate, if liked

15ml/1 tbsp dried mixed sea salad

125ml/4fl oz/½ cup natural/plain low-fat or non-dairy yogurt

175ml/6fl oz/¾ cup coconut water from a carton

If you battle with mood swings and poor concentration due to PMS and the menopause it can be helpful to include vitamin B and mineral-rich foods in your diet.

1 Scoop the passion fruit seeds into a blender goblet, then add the banana, broccoli and kale. Add the ground seed mix, goji berries and sea salad then pour in the yogurt and coconut water.

2 Screw on the lid and blitz until smooth with fine red speckles. Adjust the thickness with a little water if needed.

3 Pour into a tall glass and serve topped with a few extra chopped goji berries, if liked.

NUTRIENT NOTE – The body needs 16 essential minerals in order to function properly. The most important ones for women are: calcium needed for bones, nerves and muscles, especially important for menopausal women; iron for healthy red blood cells and to help fight fatigue; magnesium for energy release and to aid dopamine production and help the body process oestrogen; potassium to maintain fluid and electrolyte balance; selenium for healthy hair and nails; and finally zinc for efficient functioning of the immune system.

Energy 460kcal/1121kJ; Protein 14.7g; Carbohydrate 42.7g, of which sugars 33.9g; Fat 9.4g, of which saturates 2g; Cholesterol 2mg; Calcium 267mg; Fibre 5.4g; Sodium 92mg.

Hormone balance – men

Boost testosterone levels with this Mexican-inspired guacamole-style shake.

1 Put the tomato, chilli, kiwi and avocado in a blender goblet, then add the kale, ground seed mix, almonds and coconut water. Screw on the lid and blitz until smooth.

2 Pour into a glass, stir in chopped fresh coriander, and add lime juice to taste.

Serves 1

1 tomato, cut into quarters

1 slice of fresh red chilli

1 kiwi fruit, peeled and cut into chunks

½ small ripe avocado, pitted, flesh scooped from the skin

15g/½oz/½ cup shredded kale

15ml/1 tbsp ground seed mix, see p115

10 unblanched almonds

250ml/8fl oz/1 cup coconut water from a carton, or water

2–3 fresh coriander/cilantro stems, finely chopped

lime juice, to taste

SMOOTHIE TIP – This is quite a thick shake, so stir in a little extra water to get the consistency you prefer.

NUTRIENT NOTE – Dark green leafy vegetables such as kale, spinach and chard are a good source of B vitamins while the ground seeds contain zinc; both are known to boost testosterone levels. Lycopene, the carotenoid pigment that turns tomatoes red, is absorbed more readily by the body when it is eaten in conjunction with avocado or avocado oil and may help protect against prostate cancer.

Energy 400kcal/1686kJ; Protein 7.3g; Carbohydrate 56.6g, of which sugars 39.7g; Fat 6.4g, of which saturates 0.2g; Cholesterol 0mg; Calcium 77mg; Fibre 7.9g; Sodium 25mg.

Blueberry booster

Serves 1

75g/3oz/¾ cup blueberries

225g/8oz or a 5cm/2in thick wedge of watermelon, peel cut away, flesh cut into chunks

25g/1oz/1 cup baby spinach leaves

½ orange, freshly squeezed juice and the flesh scraped from the shell

10ml/2 tsp dried goji berries

NUTRIENT NOTE – Like cranberries, blueberries can be a valuable aid against recurrent urinary tract infections such as cystitis. Researchers are currently working out whether they may also help protect against worsening vision through age-related glaucoma and cataracts, but more information is needed.

This might look like an imposter in a green smoothie chapter but it is a good way to get green veg into members of the family who are anti anything green. The fruit completely masks the flavour of the spinach, while protein-boosting goji berries add an extra sweetness.

1 Put all the ingredients in a blender goblet, screw on the lid and blend until smooth with fine speckles.

2 Pour into a glass and serve.

Energy 280kcal/639kJ; Protein 3.9g; Carbohydrate 40.3g, of which sugars 34g; Fat 1.3g, of which saturates 0.3g; Cholesterol 0mg; Calcium 86mg; Fibre 5g; Sodium 43mg.

Age defier

Serves 1

75g/3oz/generous 1/4 cup blackberries

50g/2oz or 2 large strawberries, hulled

250ml/8floz/1 cup unsweetened almond milk

1 small banana, peeled and sliced

25g/1oz/1 cup baby spinach leaves

15ml/1 tbsp dried sea salad

15ml/1 tbsp dried goji berries

10ml/2 tsp ground flaxseeds

5ml/1 tsp hemp oil

This anti-ageing two-tone smoothie is just bursting with antioxidants and good omega 3 fatty acids, which are not only anti-inflammatory but are also linked to improved brain function. It is also packed with protein, vitamins and minerals to help keep your body at optimum health so that you can live life to the full for longer.

1 Put the blackberries, strawberries and 15ml/1 tbsp of the almond milk in a blender goblet, screw on the lid and blitz until smooth. Pour into the base of a glass, reserving 5ml/1 tsp, and set aside.

2 Rinse the blender goblet, then add the remaining almond milk, banana, spinach, sea salad, goji berries, flaxseeds and hemp oil. Screw on the lid and blitz until smooth.

3 Slowly pour the green smoothie into the glass over the berry base, pouring over the back of a teaspoon so that one colour sits on top of the other. Spoon dots of the remaining berry purée over the top of the smoothie to decorate, then serve.

SMOOTHIE TIP – Sea salad is sold dried and in small shreds and is a mix of dulse, nori and sea lettuce. There's no need to rehydrate it before use as it is being mixed with almond milk.

Energy 501kcal/1280kJ; Protein 8.9g; Carbohydrate 43.9g, of which sugars 35.3g; Fat 16g, of which saturates 2g; Cholesterol 0mg; Calcium 103mg; Fibre 7.2g; Sodium 207mg.

High-impact berry and kale

Mild, smooth and super-filling. While this may not be the greenest-coloured smoothie in the chapter, it is full of energy-boosting carbs and healthy fibre, antioxidants, vitamins and minerals for slow, sustained release that will keep you motivated and on target.

Serves 1

75g/3oz/¾ cup blueberries

40g/1½oz/¼ cup fresh or frozen blackberries

45ml/4 tbsp natural/plain low-fat or non-dairy yogurt

15g/½oz/½ cup shredded kale

½ ripe avocado, pitted, flesh scooped from the skin

75g/3oz/½ cup seedless green grapes

5ml/1 tsp hemp powder

10ml/2 tsp sunflower seeds

250ml/8fl oz/1 cup water

5ml/1 tsp honey or sweetener of choice

1 Put the blueberries, blackberries and yogurt in a small blender if you have one and blitz until smooth. If you only have one goblet with your machine, decant the purée into a bowl and rinse out the goblet.

2 Blend all the remaining ingredients, except for the sweetener, until smooth.

3 Pour the smoothie into a glass, sweeten to taste and adjust the consistency with a little extra water, if necessary. Drizzle the berry purée over the top and swirl it to make an attractive pattern, if you like.

SMOOTHIE TIP – Blueberries last well in the fridge but blackberries tend to go soft very quickly. Keep a handy supply of berries in the freezer, then just take out a small handful when you need them. Add them while they're still frozen for an instant way to chill your shake.

Energy 281kcal/1175kJ; Protein 6.3g; Carbohydrate 31.3g, of which sugars 25.5g; Fat 15.6g, of which saturates 3g; Cholesterol 1mg; Calcium 135mg; Fibre 8.4g; Sodium 41mg.

Super-powered bonanza

Serves 1

75g/3oz/½ cup raspberries

75g/3oz/¾ cup blueberries or blackberries

30ml/2 tbsp rolled oats

50g/2oz or 3 romaine lettuce leaves, torn into pieces

25g/1oz/1 cup shredded kale

½ banana, peeled and sliced

10ml/2 tsp dried goji berries

250ml/8fl oz/1 cup oat milk

Don't reach for the quick sugary, energy-boosting biscuits or cake. Slow-release carbs in the form of oats, berries, kale and banana make for a much healthier option as they help to stabilize blood sugar levels but also contain vital vitamins and minerals to keep us in top shape.

1 Put the berries in a blender goblet, or if you have a smaller second blender goblet, use that for preference. Screw on the lid and blitz until smooth.

2 Decant the berry purée into a small bowl if you only have one blender goblet, then rinse out the goblet.

3 Blend all the remaining ingredients together until smooth, then pour into a tall glass. Spoon the berry purée over the top and swirl together with a teaspoon or leave it as an attractive layer, as shown.

NUTRIENT NOTE – Rich in antioxidants, blueberries may help to stabilize brain function and protect neural tissue from oxidative stress. This may improve memory and learning, and even reduce the symptoms of depression.

Energy 494kcal/1539kJ; Protein 9.1g; Carbohydrate 51.6g, of which sugars 35.3g; Fat 6.8g, of which saturates 0.3g; Cholesterol 0mg; Calcium 73mg; Fibre 9.9g; Sodium 16mg.

Chamomile, melon and mint pacifier

Serves 1

1 chamomile teabag

250ml/8fl oz/1 cup boiling water

8 fresh mint leaves

225g/8oz or 1/4 green-fleshed melon, seeded, peeled and cut into chunks

25g/1oz/1 cup round/butterhead lettuce leaves, torn into pieces

SMOOTHIE TIP – Chamomile flowers have long been made into tea and are prized for their fragrant, soothing and calming properties. A teabag is the easiest way of making up this tea, but if you only have loose tea leaves use 2.5ml/½ tsp. Let them steep in the boiling water for a few minutes, but don't leave them for too long or the flavour will become bitter.

For many of us, introducing more green shakes is a way of giving our digestive system a holiday, away from the stresses of a diet loaded with caffeine, alcohol, fat, refined sugar and white flours. This soothing herb tea-based smoothie is the perfect antidote to modern living.

1 Put the teabag in a cup, pour over the boiling water and leave to infuse for 2 minutes. Remove the teabag and leave the tea to go cold.

2 Pour the cooled chamomile tea into a blender goblet, then add the mint leaves, melon and lettuce leaves. Screw on the lid and blitz until smooth. Pour into a tall glass and serve.

Energy 78kcal/330kJ; Protein 3.1g; Carbohydrate 13.5g, of which sugars 13.5g; Fat 1.6g, of which saturates 0.3g; Cholesterol 0mg; Calcium 104mg; Fibre 4.4g; Sodium 56mg.

Sleep easy

Serves 1

1 chamomile teabag
90g/3½oz iceberg lettuce
1 small banana, peeled
juice of ½ lemon

SMOOTHIE TIP – This mixture will be slightly warm from the chamomile tea. If you prefer it chilled, make it in advance and keep it in the fridge, or put ice cubes in the glass, pour over the smoothie and leave for a minute.

Some herbal teas are known for their purely soporific qualities, but this concoction is slightly more substantial. Blended bananas provide slow-release carbohydrates to sustain you through the night and lettuce is renowned for its sleep-inducing properties.

1 Cover the teabag with 150ml/¼ pint/⅔ cup boiling water and leave to steep for 10 minutes.

2 Meanwhile, chop the lettuce and banana and put both into a blender goblet. Screw on the lid and blend until smooth, scraping down from the sides of the goblet if necessary.

3 Remove the teabag, add the chamomile tea and lemon juice to the blender and blend until smooth. Pour into a glass and serve.

Energy 89kcal/376kJ; Protein 1.7g; Carbohydrate 20.1g, of which sugars 18.3g; Fat 0.7g, of which saturates 0.2g; Cholesterol 0mg; Calcium 30mg; Fibre 1.7g; Sodium 4mg.

Smoothie bowls

Smoothies are taken one step further here, served fashionably in bowls, with bright and bold fruity toppings, crisp golden granolas, crunchy chopped nuts and seeds, and sprinkles of vibrant green spirulina or wheatgrass, purple açaí powder or eye-catching goji berries. Arrange in swirls, stripes, patterns or simply sprinkle the toppings over. Bring out the artist in you and wake up the senses in every way.

Broccoli and avocado wake-up bowl

Serves 1

½ medium ripe avocado, pitted, flesh scooped from the skin

40g/1½oz or 3 small broccoli florets, plus a few extra tiny pieces, for topping

2 fresh parsley stems

10ml/2 tsp ground flaxseeds

10 unblanched almonds, plus a few extra quartered, for topping

120ml/4fl oz/½ cup cloudy pressed apple juice

juice of ¼ lime, to taste

For the topping

25g/1oz or 2 frozen chunks of mango, cut into small dice, no need to defrost

5ml/1 tsp chopped fresh parsley

1 slice of fresh red chilli, seeded, finely chopped, or to taste

1 cherry tomato, diced

a little grated lime rind

This guacamole-style smoothie combines everything you need for a breakfast: good carbs, healthy fats and a mix of vitamins and minerals, with the zing of lime and a little fiery chilli to wake up and kick-start your day.

1 Put the avocado, broccoli and parsley in a blender goblet, then add the flaxseeds, almonds and apple juice. Screw on the lid and blend until smooth.

2 Adjust with a little water if it is very thick and add lime juice to taste. Pour the smoothie into a bowl.

3 Mix the mango, chopped parsley, chilli and tomato for the topping together and sprinkle over the bowl, together with a little grated lime rind, a few tiny pieces of broccoli and quartered almonds. Serve immediately.

SMOOTHIE TIP – Chillies vary considerably in heat. As a general rule, the smaller they are the more hot and fiery they are. Test one on the tip of your tongue before deciding how much to add.
NUTRIENT NOTE – Parsley is rich in vitamin K, which works with protein to strengthen bones. It is also a good source of calcium and potassium, and also contains smaller amounts of iron and phosphorous.

Energy 328kcal/1369kJ; Protein 7.8g; Carbohydrate 22g, of which sugars 17g; Fat 23.9g, of which saturates 3.9g; Cholesterol 0mg; Calcium 66mg; Fibre 9.7g; Sodium 42mg.

Avocado and matcha tea bowl

Start the day with healthy green tea, but rather than serving it in a cup, use it as the base for this avocado, spinach and banana smoothie. If you are in a hurry, brew the tea in half the amount of boiling water, then top up with ice cubes.

Serves 1

1 matcha teabag

175ml/6fl oz/¾ cup boiling water

½ medium ripe avocado, pitted, flesh scooped from the skin

25g/1oz/1 cup baby spinach leaves

15ml/1 tbsp dried shredded sea salad

75g/3oz/½ cup frozen banana slices, no need to defrost

juice of ½ lime

For the topping

30ml/2 tbsp low-fat natural yogurt or dairy-free alternative

25g/1oz or 2 frozen mango chunks, just defrosted, diced

a few baby spinach leaves

a few pomegranate seeds

10ml/2 tsp pistachio nuts, chopped

10ml/2 tsp sunflower seeds

a large pinch of spirulina powder

1 Put the teabag in a cup, pour over the boiling water and leave to steep for 5 minutes. Remove the teabag and leave the tea to cool completely.

2 Pour the cooled tea into a blender goblet, add the avocado, spinach, sea salad, banana slices and lime juice. Screw on the lid and blitz until smooth.

3 Pour the smoothie into a bowl and add a swirl of yogurt. Top with the mango chunks and spinach leaves, then scatter with the pomegranate seeds, nuts and sunflower seeds. Finish with a sprinkle of spirulina.

SMOOTHIE TIP – To make frozen banana slices, simply slice bananas and open-freeze them on a tray lined with baking parchment. Freeze for 3 hours, until firm, then lift off the paper and place in a plastic bag. Squeeze out the air and seal the bag with a clip. Label and freeze for up to a month. Take out as many slices as you need, when you need them, and use them straight from the freezer.

NUTRIENT NOTE – Look out for packs of mixed shredded and dried dulse, nori and sea lettuce in the health food store. They are rich in iodine, which is needed for normal functioning of the thyroid gland, with smaller amounts of copper and iron for healthy blood, magnesium for muscles and nerves, calcium for healthy bones, potassium for fluid balance and zinc for the body's immune system.

Energy 364kcal/1518kJ; Protein 8.5g; Carbohydrate 28.8g, of which sugars 22.4g; Fat 24.6g, of which saturates 4.5g; Cholesterol 0mg; Calcium 111mg; Fibre 7.4g; Sodium 49mg.

Gorgeous green bowl

Serves 1

15g/½oz/½ cup shredded kale

25g/1oz/1 cup baby spinach leaves

1 apple, peeled, cored and roughly chopped

½ medium ripe avocado, pitted, flesh scooped from the skin

½ small pear, no need to peel, cored and sliced

1 kiwi fruit, peeled and sliced

125ml/4fl oz/½ cup unsweetened almond milk

For the topping

15ml/1 tbsp alfalfa sprouts

10ml/2 tsp pumpkin seeds

5ml/1 tsp dried goji berries

This vibrant green bowl just screams out that it is good for you. It is packed with energy-boosting avocado and pear for a velvety smoothness, plus antioxidant-, mineral- and vitamin-boosting green leaves and kiwi, to enhance immunity and health.

1 Put the kale, spinach and apple in a blender goblet, then add half the avocado, pear and kiwi. Pour in the almond milk, screw on the lid and blitz until smooth.

2 Pour the smoothie into a bowl. Slice the remaining avocado, pear and kiwi, then arrange over the top of the smoothie. Add the alfalfa sprouts to the middle, then sprinkle with the seeds and goji berries and serve.

SMOOTHIE TIP – Sprouting seeds make great toppings for smoothie bowls. As the seeds begin to sprout, their natural nutrients increase massively to meet the growing needs of the young shoots, making them nutrient-dense yet easy to digest. Buy ready-sprouted one in small packs in the supermarket or grow your own at home.

Energy 337kcal/1133kJ; Protein 6.6g; Carbohydrate 21.9g, of which sugars 18.1g; Fat 19.6g, of which saturates 3.6g; Cholesterol 0mg; Calcium 95mg; Fibre 8.6g; Sodium 135mg.

Tropical sensation in a bowl

Adding a mixture of fresh and frozen fruit to a smoothie gives a texture like soft scoop ice cream, which is deliciously refreshing and helps to cut down on the amount of prep needed. There is no need to defrost frozen fruit first – just add a handful to the blender and away you go.

Serves 1

1 kiwi fruit, peeled and chopped

50g/2oz/⅓ cup frozen banana slices, no need to defrost

50g/2oz or 4 frozen mango chunks, no need to defrost

4 little gem lettuce leaves

125ml/4fl oz/½ cup coconut water from a carton

2.5ml/½ tsp wheatgrass powder

For the topping

1 frozen ice cube of raspberry purée, see p24, defrosted

25g/1oz or 2 frozen mango chunks, just defrosted, diced

a few raspberries

a few hulled hemp seeds

a few tiny feathery rocket/arugula leaves or a little shredded lettuce

1 Reserve one-quarter of the kiwi fruit for the topping and put the rest in a blender goblet with the banana slices, mango chunks and lettuce.

2 Pour in the coconut water and add the wheatgrass powder. Screw on the lid and blend until smooth.

3 Pour the smoothie into a bowl. Decorate the top with a swirl of raspberry purée, the remaining kiwi fruit, diced mango and a few whole raspberries. Sprinkle with the hemp seeds and rocket or lettuce and serve.

SMOOTHIE TIP - Mangoes, cherries and summer berry fruits are readily available frozen in the supermarket, or make up your own fruit packs – see p24. Freeze these fruits for up to 6 months.
NUTRIENT NOTE - Mangoes are packed with immune-boosting vitamin C, while the phenolic and carotene compounds they contain are thought to protect against some forms of cancer and aid heart health. Beta-carotene also boosts eye health while the soluble fibre mangoes contain helps to slow down the release of energy from the naturally occurring fruit sugar.

Energy 124kcal/527kJ; Protein 2g; Carbohydrate 29.3g, of which sugars 27.7g; Fat 0.6g, of which saturates 0.1g; Cholesterol 0mg; Calcium 31mg; Fibre 5.4g; Sodium 5mg.

Spinach and spirulina smoothie bowl

This smoothie bowl has one of the most striking colours – a bold, deep green from antioxidant-rich spinach and kale – and is then supercharged with protein-boosting spirulina and mineral-rich sea salad. Adding some banana helps to sweeten and balance the kale, which can sometimes be a little strong for some people's tastes.

Serves 1

25g/1oz/1 cup baby spinach leaves

15g/½oz/½ cup shredded kale

1 small banana, peeled and sliced

125ml/4fl oz/½ cup pressed cloudy apple juice

1.5ml/¼ tsp spirulina, plus a little extra, to decorate

15ml/1 tbsp dried sea salad, plus a little extra, to decorate

For the topping

50g/2oz or about 2 large strawberries, hulled and sliced

5ml/1 tsp sunflower seeds

5ml/1 tsp hemp oil

1 Put the spinach and kale in a blender goblet with half the sliced banana. Pour in the apple juice, then add the spirulina and dried sea salad. Screw on the lid and blend until smooth.

2 Pour into a bowl, then decorate the top with the remaining sliced banana and strawberries. Sprinkle with a little extra spirulina and sea salad and the sunflower seeds, then drizzle with the hemp oil. Serve immediately.

SMOOTHIE TIP – Kale can be a little overpowering, mixing with a little naturally sweet banana helps to balance and complement the flavours.

NUTRIENT NOTE – Spinach and kale contain a high concentration of carotenoids; spinach has beta-carotene and lutein and kale has lutein and zeaxanthin. These appear to have important antioxidant properties.

Energy 215kcal/908kJ; Protein 3.6g; Carbohydrate 38.6g, of which sugars 35.4g; Fat 6.1g, of which saturates 0.9g; Cholesterol 0mg; Calcium 92mg; Fibre 3.3g; Sodium 61mg.

Papaya and orange wake-up bowl

Serves 1

½ small papaya, seeds discarded, peeled and diced (prepared weight about 100g/3¾oz)

75g/3oz or ½ carrot, scrubbed and sliced

10ml/2 tsp ground flaxseeds

juice of 1 medium orange

For the topping

30ml/2 tbsp muesli base, see p219

4 unblanched almonds, halved

50g/2oz or about 2 large strawberries, hulled and sliced

a few blueberries

SMOOTHIE TIP – If you have some frozen cubes of fruit purée, see p24, you could defrost one and drizzle it over the smoothie before serving.

Awaken the senses with this taste bonanza: creamy, smooth papaya with the tang of fresh citrus, topped with crunchy muesli and summer berries. A picture in a bowl.

1 Put the papaya, carrot, flaxseeds and orange juice in a blender goblet. Screw on the lid and blitz until smooth.

2 Pour into a bowl and decorate with the muesli base, almonds, strawberries and blueberries, then serve.

NUTRIENT NOTE – Half a papaya contains an adult's daily allowance of vitamin C, which is needed to produce white blood cells to help fight infection and to produce collagen for healthy muscles, skin and bones.

Energy 286kcal/1198kJ; Protein 8.6g; Carbohydrate 37.2g, of which sugars 22.8g; Fat 12.3g, of which saturates 1.2g; Cholesterol 0mg; Calcium 91mg; Fibre 11.3g; Sodium 68mg.

Buckwheat berry blast bowl

Buckwheat adds a high-fibre and mineral boost to this healthy smoothie bowl. Look out for this tiny triangular nutty-tasting ingredient in the health food store. Soak in cold water overnight to soften, then blend with fresh berries and spinach for an alternative to bircher muesli or porridge.

1 Drain the buckwheat and put in a blender goblet. Reserve a few of the berries and add the rest to the goblet with the spinach, banana, almond butter and milk. Screw on the lid and blend until smooth, adding a little water if needed.

2 Pour into a bowl and decorate with the reserved berries, the pumpkin seeds and açaí berry powder and serve.

Serves 1

40g/1½oz/¼ cup buckwheat groats, soaked overnight in cold water

50g/2oz/½ cup blueberries

50g/2oz/⅓ cup raspberries

15g/½oz/½ cup baby spinach leaves

½ small banana, peeled and sliced

10ml/2 tsp almond butter

125ml/4fl oz/½ cup unsweetened almond milk

For the topping

5ml/1 tsp pumpkin seeds

2.5ml/½ tsp açaí berry powder

Energy 373kcal/1574kJ; Protein 10.9g; Carbohydrate 56.5g, of which sugars 20.9g; Fat 13.8g, of which saturates 1.2g; Cholesterol 0mg; Calcium 65mg; Fibre 10.3g; Sodium 121mg.

Raspberry and watermelon bowl

Rehydrate with this fab fruity and refreshing smoothie bowl that has just a hint of energy-boosting beetroot.

1 Reserve a few of the raspberries and a little of the watermelon for the topping, then put the rest in a blender goblet with the beetroot, flaxseeds and baobab powder.

2 Screw on the lid and blitz until smooth, stirring and scraping down from the sides of the goblet once or twice.

3 Spoon into a bowl and add small dots of cashew cream. Top with the reserved raspberries and watermelon, then the baby kale leaves, and scatter over a few sunflower seeds.

Serves 1

75g/3oz/½ cup raspberries

200g/7oz or 1 small slice of watermelon, peeled, most of the black seeds removed, diced

75g/3oz or 1 small beetroot/beet, scrubbed, trimmed and diced

10ml/2 tsp ground flaxseeds

5ml/1 tsp baobab powder

For the topping

10ml/2 tsp cashew cream, see p216

a few tiny baby kale leaves

a few sunflower seeds

Energy 186kcal/791kJ; Protein 5.8g; Carbohydrate 27.5g, of which sugars 23.6g; Fat 6.8g, of which saturates 3g; Cholesterol 0mg; Calcium 49mg; Fibre 8.7g; Sodium 86mg.

Açaí berry blitz bowl

Serves 1

100g/3¾oz frozen açaí berry purée (see Smoothie Tip), defrosted in the microwave for a few minutes to soften slightly

½ small banana, peeled and sliced

15g/½oz/½ cup shredded kale

30ml/2 tbsp rolled oats

125ml/4fl oz/½ cup coconut water from a carton

For the topping

30ml/2 tbsp cashew cream, see p216

a few blueberries

a few raspberries

5ml/1 tsp dried goji berries

a pinch of moringa, wheatgrass or spirulina powder

a few hulled hemp seeds

a few hulled pumpkin seeds

Açaí (pronounced 'ah-sah-ee') has grown in popularity as a must-have superfood. These small, dark purple fruits come from the açaí palm tree, which is found in the Amazonian regions of Brazil. Buy as a frozen purée, defrost in the microwave and then purée with kale and banana for this antioxidant-boosting breakfast.

1 Put the açaí purée, banana and kale in a blender goblet, then add the rolled oats and coconut water. Screw on the lid and blitz until smooth.

2 Pour into a bowl. Top with small blobs of the cashew cream in a ring, then add the blueberries and raspberries, sprinkle with the goji berries, moringa, wheatgrass or spirulina powder, add the seeds, and serve.

SMOOTHIE TIP – You can buy açaí purée in the freezer sections of good health food stores but if you can't find it, use 100g/3¾oz/¾ cup frozen pitted cherries instead. There's no need to defrost these fully if your blender is the kind that is tough enough to blitz ice cubes. Açaí berries can also be found in little packets of powder, which add a bright splash of colour when sprinkled over a green or orange smoothie bowl.

NUTRIENT NOTE – There are some wild claims being made about the health benefits of açaí berries, from anti-ageing to weight loss. There is little evidence to back this up but they do contain vitamin C and also anthocyanins, which give them their colour; these antioxidants are also found in blueberries and cranberries and are thought to help protect the body from free-radical damage.

Energy 321kcal/1347kJ; Protein 7.7g; Carbohydrate 42.3g, of which sugars 18.3g; Fat 14.6g, of which saturates 9.1g; Cholesterol 0mg; Calcium 85mg; Fibre 9.6g; Sodium 30mg.

Strawberry and chia crush bowl

Pretty and pink, this smoothie bowl has a hidden punch with the addition of lemon – zingy rind, pith and juicy flesh included – to create a fresh taste that will remind you of summer lemonade. Use ripe strawberries, when they are in season, or else you could use frozen ones and thaw them.

Serves 1

150g/5oz/1½ cups strawberries, hulled

1 small banana, peeled and sliced

¼ lemon, diced

2.5ml/½ tsp chia seeds

For the topping

30ml/2 tbsp low-fat natural yogurt or dairy-free alternative

5ml/1 tsp hulled hemp seeds

a few extra chia seeds

1.5ml/¼ tsp açaí powder (optional)

1 Reserve a strawberry and half the banana slices for the topping. Put the rest in a blender goblet with the lemon. Screw on the lid and blend until smooth. Sprinkle in the chia seeds, then screw on the lid and blitz again until smooth.

2 Pour into a bowl and swirl in the yogurt. Top with the reserved strawberry, cut into slices, and the remaining banana slices, then sprinkle with the hemp seeds, extra chia seeds and a little açaí powder, if using. Serve.

SMOOTHIE TIP - Açaí powder can be bought in small sachets from a health food store. It is rich in vitamin C and is mauve in colour, which quickly darkens when in contact with moisture.
NUTRIENT NOTE - Strawberries contain more vitamin C than any of the other red summer berries. Although naturally sweet they contain just 27 calories per 100g/3¾oz.

Energy 153kcal/647kJ; Protein 4.8g; Carbohydrate 30.7g, of which sugars 27.1g; Fat 2g, of which saturates 0.2g; Cholesterol 0mg; Calcium 76mg; Fibre 5.3g; Sodium 46mg.

Blueberry and vanilla smoothie bowl

Serves 1

75g/3oz/¾ cup fresh or frozen blueberries, no need to defrost

½ small banana, peeled and sliced

15g/½oz/½ cup baby spinach leaves

15ml/1 tbsp rolled oats

15ml/1 tbsp sunflower seeds

5ml/1 tsp maca powder

125ml/4fl oz/½ cup unsweetened almond milk

a few drops of vanilla extract

For the topping

30ml/2 tbsp cashew cream, see p216

1 fresh fig, cut into thin wedges

30ml/2 tbsp fresh or frozen blueberries, just defrosted if frozen

5ml/1 tsp dried goji berries

This sumptuous bowl is dairy free, yet you certainly don't feel as though you are missing out with the creamy blueberry and banana vanilla-flavoured smoothie. Boosted with healthy oats, seeds and maca, it is then topped with homemade cashew cream for a luxurious start to the day.

1 Put the frozen blueberries, banana and spinach in a blender goblet, then add the oats, sunflower seeds and maca powder. Pour in the almond milk and vanilla extract, then screw on the lid and blend until smooth.

2 Pour into a bowl and top with the cashew cream, fig wedges, extra blueberries and goji berries, and serve.

SMOOTHIE TIP – Vary the toppings to suit what you have in the fridge or freezer. A mixture of summer berries or sliced peaches would also taste great.

NUTRIENT NOTE – Blueberries are often called a superfood, because they are rich in antioxidants, including anthocyanins, which give them their blue colour. They are naturally sweet and bursting with vitamin K and C, plus they contain manganese, which helps the body process cholesterol, carbohydrates, protein and phenolic compounds. Maca powder is ground from a Peruvian root vegetable, high in antioxidants and minerals, particularly iron. It is recommended you do not exceed a teaspoon a day.

Energy 459kcal/1650kJ; Protein 8.6g; Carbohydrate 50.6g, of which sugars 30g; Fat 20.6g, of which saturates 10g; Cholesterol 0mg; Calcium 64mg; Fibre 7.4g; Sodium 113mg.

Bowl of cherryaid

Frozen ready-prepared cherries make a great healthy addition to this amazingly coloured deep-red smoothie. There's no need to defrost them first, just blitz with beetroot, kale and a hint of cinnamon for a vitalizing and energy-boosting bowl.

Serves 1

110g/3¾oz fresh or frozen pitted cherries

100g/3½oz or 1 medium beetroot/beet, peeled, trimmed and diced

15g/½oz/½ cup shredded kale

a large pinch of ground cinnamon

125ml/4fl oz/½ cup water

For the topping

5ml/1 tsp sunflower seeds

5ml/1 tsp ground flaxseeds

5ml/1 tsp dried goji berries

10ml/2 tsp rolled oats

a few blueberries

a few sun-dried mulberries (optional)

a few tiny edible flowers such as violas or herb flowers (optional)

1 Put the cherries, beetroot, kale, cinnamon and water in a blender goblet. Screw on the lid and blitz until smooth.

2 Pour the smoothie into a bowl and top with the seeds, goji berries, oats and then the blueberries. Decorate with mulberries and flowers, if using, and serve.

SMOOTHIE TIP – Look out for mulberries in sealed pouches in the health food store. They look a little like a dried brown raspberry but add a great natural sweet hit to any smoothie bowl.
NUTRIENT NOTE – Beetroot is a powerhouse of antioxidants and nutrients. It includes the folates that are vital for new cell growth and DNA, which are so important for pregnant women, along with other B vitamins and small amounts of vitamin C, plus the minerals iron, manganese, copper and magnesium with smaller amounts of potassium. The good carbs will help to fight fatigue and boost energy. The pigment betacyanin gives beetroot its deep red colour and works with manganese and vitamin C to aid good eye health and overall tissue health and may even help to reduce the oxidation of LDL cholesterol, so helping to reduce the risk of heart disease.

Energy 254kcal/854kJ; Protein 7.5g; Carbohydrate 36g, of which sugars 25.3g; Fat 5.2g, of which saturates 0.6g; Cholesterol 0mg; Calcium 78mg; Fibre 7.4g; Sodium 110mg.

Carrot cake in a bowl

Serves 1

115g/4oz or 1 small carrot, scrubbed and diced

1 dessert apple, cored but not peeled, diced

1 slice of fresh root ginger, no need to peel, quartered

a pinch of ground cinnamon

125ml/4fl oz/½ cup water

15ml/1 tbsp cashew cream, see below

For the topping

15ml/1 tbsp cashew cream, see below

40g/1½oz/⅓ cup fruity granola

1 Medjool date, pitted and sliced

50g/2oz or ½ small carrot, scrubbed and pared into thin ribbons with a vegetable peeler

A twist on the traditional carrot cake, this easy-to-make smoothie bowl is a great way to include two portions of the recommended dose of fruit and veg for the day without even trying. It also happens to be pretty, and delicious!

1 Put the carrot, apple, ginger and cinnamon in a blender goblet. Pour in the water and add the cashew cream, then screw on the lid and blend until smooth.

2 Pour the mixture into a bowl. Thin the cashew cream for the topping with a little water, then swirl it over the smoothie. Sprinkle with the fruity granola and the sliced date, then top with the carrot ribbons and serve.

SMOOTHIE TIP – If you don't have any cashew cream then you can instead add 4 unblanched almonds to the smoothie base with a little extra water, and top with a spoonful of plain/natural low-fat yogurt, mixed with half a mashed banana or flavoured with a little finely chopped fresh root ginger.

NUTRIENT NOTE – Carrots have tough cellular walls but blending helps to make them easier for the body to digest and convert the beta-carotene they contain into vitamin A. This helps to maintain good health, nourish the skin and fight the signs of ageing. Herbalists believe carrots have detoxifying properties.

CASHEW CREAM

Makes 250g/9oz/generous 1 cup

150g/5oz/1 cup cashew nut pieces
a few drops of vanilla extract
10ml/2 tsp maple syrup or sweetener of choice

1 Add the cashews to a bowl and pour over cold water to generously cover the nuts. Cover the bowl with a plate and chill in the fridge or a cool place overnight. Drain the nuts in a colander, reserving the water.

2 Put the nuts and 60ml/4 tbsp of the soaking water in a blender goblet. Screw on the lid and blitz until smooth. You may need to scrape down from the sides of the blender goblet once or twice and if very thick, add in a little extra soaking water to get a really smooth cream. Add the vanilla and sweetener and blend briefly together.

3 Spoon into a jar, smooth the surface, then screw or clip on the lid. Chill in the fridge for up to 3 days if not using immediately.

Bowl: Energy 328kcal/1380kJ; Protein 5.4g; Carbohydrate 57.2g, of which sugars 44g; Fat 10.1g, of which saturates 5.2g; Cholesterol 0mg; Calcium 78mg; Fibre 10.2g; Sodium 70mg.
Cream: Energy 177kcal/758kJ; Protein 4.8g; Carbohydrate 38.1g, of which sugars 37.8g; Fat 1.8g, of which saturates 0.5g; Cholesterol 0mg; Calcium 142mg; Fibre 8.6g; Sodium 158mg.

Apple and blackberry crumble bowl

This pale-coloured bowl contains all the flavours of apple crumble but with none of the refined carbs. Instead, it is made with healthy homemade high-fibre, high-energy nut muesli and soothing low-fat natural yogurt.

Serves 1

1 dessert apple, no need to peel, quartered, cored, dice 3/4 and slice 1/4

1 small ripe pear, no need to peel, cored and diced

125g/4 1/4oz/1/2 cup low-fat natural/plain yogurt

a few drops of vanilla extract

For the topping

40g/1 1/2oz/1/3 cup nut muesli, see below

1 frozen ice cube of blackberry purée, see p24, defrosted

a few blackberries

1 Put the diced apple, pear, yogurt and vanilla in a blender goblet, screw on the lid and blend until smooth. Pour into a bowl.

2 Spoon the muesli into the middle of the bowl. Top with the apple slices. Spoon dots of blackberry purée on the smoothie bowl, sprinkle with a few extra blackberries and serve.

SMOOTHIE TIP – Apples and pears quickly go brown so make sure you serve this smoothie bowl the moment you have made it.
NUTRIENT NOTE – Apples and pears are rich in pectin, the setting agent in jam that also helps to remove bad cholesterol from the body. They also stimulate the growth of friendly bacteria in the large intestine, boost vitamin C and contain the simple sugar fructose, which is sweeter than sucrose found in sugar cane but is metabolized by the body more slowly.

MUESLI BASE

Makes 350g/12oz/3 1/2 cups

- 100g/3 3/4oz/1 cup jumbo rolled oats
- 75g/3oz/3/4 cup barley flakes
- 75g/3oz/3/4 cup rye flakes
- 50g/2oz/1/2 cup quinoa flakes
- 60ml/4 tbsp/1/4 cup ground flaxseeds
- 60ml/4 tbsp/1/4 cup sunflower seeds
- 60ml/4 tbsp/1/4 cup pumpkin seeds

1 Put all the ingredients in a large mixing bowl and mix together. Spoon into a jar, screw or clip on the lid and store in a cool place for up to 2 weeks.

NUT MUESLI

Makes 275g/10oz/2 1/4 cups

- 175g/6oz/1 1/2 cups muesli base
- 15g/1/2oz/1/4 cup desiccated/dry unsweetened shredded coconut
- 40g/1 1/2oz/1/4 cup Brazil nuts, roughly chopped
- 40g/1 1/2oz/1/4 cup unblanched almonds, roughly chopped

1 Put all the ingredients in a large mixing bowl and mix together. Spoon into a jar, screw or clip on the lid and store in a cool place for up to 2 weeks.

Bowl: Energy 308kcal/1302kJ; Protein 13.7g; Carbohydrate 48.3g, of which sugars 26.1g; Fat 8g, of which saturates 0.9g; Cholesterol 0mg; Calcium 236mg; Fibre 7.4g; Sodium 105mg.
Base: Energy 442kcal/1859kJ; Protein 15.9g; Carbohydrate 55.4g, of which sugars 0.7g; Fat 18.9g, of which saturates 2.0g; Cholesterol 0mg; Calcium 52mg; Fibre 7.9g; Sodium 31mg (per 100g).
Nut: Energy 512kcal/2136kJ; Protein 15.8g; Carbohydrate 37.8g, of which sugars 1.8g; Fat 34.0g, of which saturates 7.5g; Cholesterol 0mg; Calcium 96mg; Fibre 6.3g; Sodium 24mg (per 100g).

Cacao and cherry bowl

Serves 1

25g/1oz/¼ cup cashew nut pieces

50ml/2fl oz/¼ cup boiling water

100g/3¾oz/¾ cup frozen pitted cherries, no need to defrost

40g/1½oz/generous ¼ cup frozen sliced banana, no need to defrost

40g/1½oz/1 stem purple sprouting broccoli with leaves, sliced

5ml/1 tsp raw cacao powder

125ml/4fl oz/½ cup cold water

For the topping

30ml/2 tbsp muesli base, see p219

5ml/1 tsp dried goji berries

1 fresh or frozen cherry, pitted and quartered

1 frozen cube of strawberry purée, defrosted, see p24

Frozen fruits save time when smoothie making and mean that you always have healthy ingredients at the ready. Keep a jar of homemade muesli in the cupboard and this energizing breakfast can be put together in minutes.

1 Soak the cashew nuts in a heatproof bowl with boiling water for 5 minutes to soften them slightly. Put the nuts and soaking water in a blender goblet with the frozen cherries and banana, the broccoli and the cacao powder.

2 Add half the cold water, screw on the lid and blend until smooth. Adjust the consistency with extra water as needed.

3 Pour into a bowl. Top with the muesli base, goji berries and cherry, then drizzle with a little strawberry purée and serve.

NUTRIENT NOTE – Raw cacao powder comes from cacao beans that have been dried at low temperatures rather than being roasted and so contain flavonoid antioxidants that may help protect the body from free-radical damage. As well as containing protein, fibre, vitamins and essential vitamins, raw cacao also contains a natural mood enhancer.

Energy 409kcal/1442kJ; Protein 11.9g; Carbohydrate 41.7g, of which sugars 24.7g; Fat 16.9g, of which saturates 3.2g; Cholesterol 0mg; Calcium 60mg; Fibre 6.4g; Sodium 34mg.

Cacao and banana maple bowl

A rich, dark chocolatey fix, this smoothie bowl is made with almond milk and is packed with protein boosters, and topped with an easy maple-glazed seed brittle for a crunchy mineral-rich finish. It is ideal after a workout as an alternative to a protein bar.

Serves 1

1 small banana, peeled and sliced
20ml/4 tsp vanilla protein powder
10ml/2 tsp raw cacao powder
10ml/2 tsp ground flaxseeds
2 tsp cashew or hazelnut butter
25g/1oz/1 cup baby spinach leaves or shredded red chard
90ml/3fl oz/⅓ cup unsweetened almond milk

For the topping

5ml/1 tsp dried goji berries
½ quantity maple-glazed seed brittle, see below

1 Reserve half the banana slices for decoration, then put the rest in a blender goblet with the protein powder, cacao, flaxseeds and nut butter.

2 Add the spinach or chard and almond milk, screw on the lid and blend until smooth.

3 Pour into a bowl, then top with the reserved banana slices, goji berries and maple-glazed seeds, and serve.

NUTRIENT NOTE – If you are on a dairy-free diet make sure that you check the label on the vanilla protein powder, as some can be whey- or dairy-based.

MAPLE-GLAZED SEED BRITTLE
Makes 2 portions

15ml/1 tbsp sunflower seeds
15ml/1 tbsp pumpkin seeds
15ml/1 tbsp sesame seeds
20ml/4 tsp maple syrup

1 Put the seeds in a small, dry frying pan and toast for 2–3 minutes, until beginning to colour.
2 Add the maple syrup and cook for a minute or two more, stirring until the syrup is bubbling and the sesame seeds are golden.
3 Tip out on to a baking sheet lined with baking parchment and spread into a thin layer. Leave to cool and harden for 15 minutes or longer, then break into pieces. Store leftovers in a container for up to 3 days.

Energy 297kcal/1250kJ; Protein 22.4g; Carbohydrate 29.5g, of which sugars 23.3g; Fat 10.3g, of which saturates 1.2g; Cholesterol 0mg; Calcium 54mg; Fibre 6.7g; Sodium 158mg.

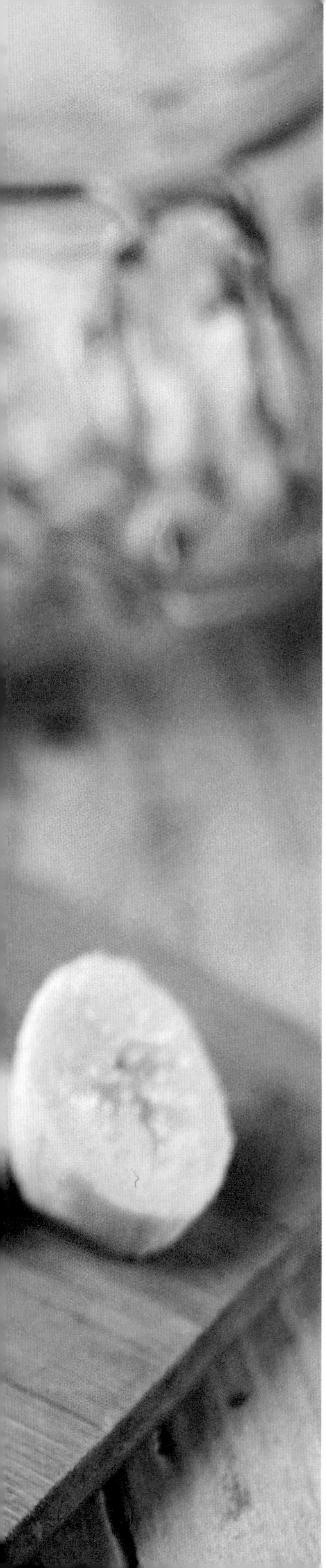

Shakes and iced drinks

Occasionally, everyone fancies a treat. Creamy, silky shakes and cooling slushes and crushes made with nutritious fruits, nuts and grains as well as more indulgent ingredients are a great option as a replacement for a dessert or sweet snack. Some are made with non-dairy ingredients, while others include dairy milk, cream, yogurt and ice cream. Most types are fairly interchangeable, meaning these irrestistible drinks are a tempting option for everyone. Just don't drink them every day!

Real vanilla milkshake

This is a milkshake for connoisseurs: nothing beats the flavour achieved by infusing a vanilla pod in the milk, although you could use a teaspoon of vanilla extract.

1 Score the vanilla pod down the middle. Place in a pan, add the milk and bring slowly to the boil. Remove from the heat but leave the pod in the milk. Leave to stand until the milk has cooled.

2 Remove the vanilla pod from the milk and scrape out the seeds with the tip of a knife. Put the seeds in a blender goblet with the milk and cream. Screw on the lid and blend until combined.

3 Add the ice cream to the mixture and blend well until it is thick and frothy. Pour the shake into two large glasses and serve immediately.

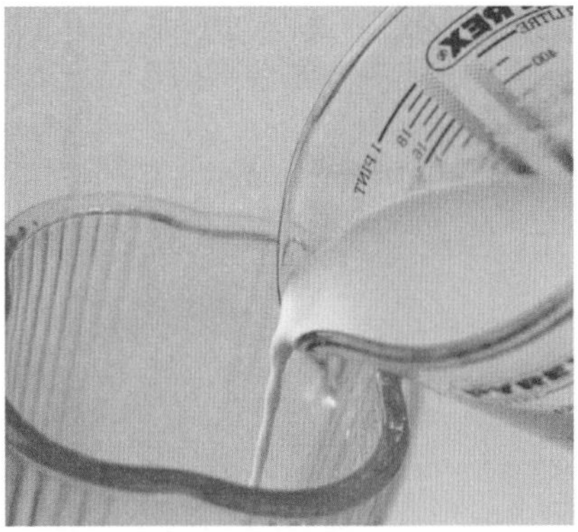

Serves 2

1 vanilla pod/bean

600ml/1 pint/2½ cups full-fat/whole milk

2 scoops of vanilla ice cream

SHAKE TIP – This classic milkshake is extremely rich and creamy. If you'd prefer a lighter consistency, replace half the cream with the same quantity of extra milk.

Energy 648kcal/2687kJ; Protein 15.8g; Carbohydrate 36.4g, of which sugars 36.3g; Fat 49.6g, of which saturates 30.8g; Cholesterol 83mg; Calcium 475mg; Fibre 0g; Sodium 205mg.

Simply strawberry shake

Serves 2

400g/14oz/3½ cups strawberries, plus extra to decorate

30–45ml/2–3 tbsp icing/ confectioners' sugar

200g/7oz/scant 1 cup Greek/ strained plain yogurt

60ml/4 tbsp single/light cream

SHAKE TIP – You can replace the strawberries with other fruits if they are not in season. Try using bananas instead to make another very popular milkshake.

Nothing evokes a sense of summer well-being more than the scent and flavour of sweet, juicy strawberries. This recipe uses an abundance of these fruits so, if possible, make it when the season is right and local ones are plentiful.

1 Hull the strawberries and place them in a blender goblet with 30ml/2 tbsp of the icing sugar. Screw on the lid and blend until smooth, scraping down from the sides of the goblet if necessary.

2 Add the yogurt and cream and blend again until smooth and frothy. Check the sweetness, adding more sugar if required.

3 Pour the milkshake into two glasses and serve decorated with extra strawberries.

Energy 286kcal/1195kJ; Protein 9.1g; Carbohydrate 30.4g, of which sugars 30.4g; Fat 16.2g, of which saturates 8.9g; Cholesterol 17mg; Calcium 217mg; Fibre 2.2g; Sodium 93mg.

Stem ginger and pear shake

Canned fruit is a good store-cupboard stand-by for when you've run out of fresh. Preserved stem ginger makes the perfect partner to pears in this creamy creation.

1 Shave off some wafer-thin slices from one of the pieces of ginger and reserve. Roughly chop the remaining ginger. Drain the pears, reserving about 150ml/¼ pint/⅔ cup of the juice.

2 Put the pears, measured juice and chopped ginger in a blender goblet. Screw on the lid and blend until smooth, scraping the mixture down from the sides of the goblet if necessary.

3 Strain the mixture into a jug or pitcher. Whisk in the milk, cream and ginger syrup and pour the shake into two glasses. Serve topped with ginger shavings.

Serves 2

3 pieces (about 65g/2½oz) of preserved stem ginger, plus 30ml/2 tbsp ginger syrup from the jar

400g/14oz can pears in natural fruit juice

150ml/1¼ pint/⅔ cup full-fat/whole milk

100ml/3½fl oz/scant ½ cup single/light cream

ice cubes

Energy 257kcal/1077kJ; Protein 4.8g; Carbohydrate 33.4g, of which sugars 33.4g; Fat 12.5g, of which saturates 8g; Cholesterol 38mg; Calcium 148mg; Fibre 2.8g; Sodium 94mg.

Dairy-free honey and banana shake

This drink demonstrates just how smooth and rich a milkshake can be, even without using dairy produce. Make it using either soya or rice milk, or any milk of your choice.

Serves 2

2 ripe bananas, peeled, plus 1 banana, peeled and sliced, to decorate

30ml/2 tbsp clear honey

15ml/1 tbsp lemon juice

300ml/1½ pint/1¼ cups soya or rice milk

4 scoops of vanilla iced non-dairy dessert

1 Break the bananas into pieces and put them in a blender goblet with the honey and lemon juice.

2 Screw on the lid and blend until very smooth, scraping the mixture down from the sides of the goblet if necessary.

3 Add the soya or rice milk and two scoops of iced cream, then blend until smooth.

4 Pour into two tall glasses and add another scoop of iced cream to each. Top with banana slices and serve immediately.

SHAKE TIP – For a dairy milkshake, you can of course use ordinary milk and vanilla ice cream.

Energy 416kcal/1749kJ; Protein 6.1g; Carbohydrate 68.4g, of which sugars 65.6g; Fat 15g, of which saturates 8.9g; Cholesterol 10mg; Calcium 117mg; Fibre 2.3g; Sodium 81mg.

Prune and apple soya shake

Serves 1

2 small eating apples, no need to peel or core

5 ready-to-eat pitted prunes

juice of 1 orange

60ml/4 tbsp soya milk

ice cubes

SMOOTHIE TIP – The sweetness of this drink will depend on the type of apple you use, so feel free to experiment.

Prunes, apples, oranges and soya milk may seem like an unusual combination but the results are fabulous. Sweet, caramel-rich and very drinkable, this is a great milkshake for both adults and children, and, of course, for anyone on a dairy-free diet. Regular cow's milk can be used, if you prefer.

1 Press half the apple through a juicer, followed by the prunes and the remaining apple.

2 Pour the apple and prune juice into a blender goblet with the orange juice and milk. Screw on the lid and blitz until smooth.

3 Pour the shake into a small glass containing a few ice cubes and serve immediately.

Pear and grape shake

Serves 1

1 large pear, no need to peel or core

150g/5oz/1 cup seedless green grapes

15ml/1 tbsp wheatgerm

60ml/4 tbsp soya yogurt

ice cubes

For a truly refreshing combination, you can't do much better than a mixture of juicy pears and grapes. Wheatgerm adds body for a sustained energy fix and soya yogurt turns the juice into a protein-packed milkshake with a lusciously light and frothy topping. This is quite a filling drink and a useful choice for those who feel that their life is too busy to prepare nutritious food. A quick and easy drink that is good for you too – what could be better?

1 Cut the pear in half. Press one half through a juicer, followed by the grapes and then the remaining pear half. Transfer the juice to a blender goblet.

2 Add the wheatgerm and yogurt to the goblet, screw on the lid and blitz until the mixture is light and frothy. Pour the milkshake into a glass containing ice cubes and serve immediately.

Soya: Energy 248kcal/1059kJ; Protein 5.1g; Carbohydrate 56.7g, of which sugars 56.7g; Fat 1.6g, of which saturates 0.2g; Cholesterol 0mg; Calcium 55mg; Fibre 9g; Sodium 39mg.

Pear: Energy 247kcal/1048kJ; Protein 8.1g; Carbohydrate 47.1g, of which sugars 42.8g; Fat 2.8g, of which saturates 0.6g; Cholesterol 1mg; Calcium 44mg; Fibre 6.7g; Sodium 8mg.

Apple and yogurt shake

While a good-quality vanilla extract is perfectly acceptable for flavouring drinks, a far more aromatic taste will be achieved using a vanilla pod. This simple shake is deliciously scented, creamy and thick, and well worth the extravagance of using a whole vanilla pod. Its lovely, snowy whiteness is delightfully speckled with tiny black vanilla seeds.

Serves 2–3

1 vanilla pod/bean

25g/1oz/2 tbsp caster/superfine sugar

3 eating apples

300g/11oz/1⅓ cups natural/plain yogurt

1 Using the tip of a sharp knife, split open the vanilla pod lengthways. Put it in a small pan with the sugar and 75ml/5 tbsp water. Heat until the sugar dissolves, then boil for 1 minute. Remove the pan from the heat and leave the syrup to steep and cool for 10 minutes.

2 Cut the apples into large chunks and push them through a juicer, then pour the juice into a blender goblet.

3 Lift the vanilla pod out of the pan and scrape the tiny black seeds back into the syrup. Pour into the goblet.

4 Add the yogurt to the goblet. Screw on the lid and blitz until the shake is thick and frothy. Chill if necessary, pour into two or three glasses and serve.

SHAKE TIP – Like most shakes, this one should ideally be served well chilled. Either use apples and yogurt straight from the fridge, or chill briefly before serving. To make a thick, icy version, you could try using frozen yogurt.

Energy 124kcal/527kJ; Protein 5.4g; Carbohydrate 25.1g, of which sugars 25.1g; Fat 1.1g, of which saturates 0.5g; Cholesterol 1mg; Calcium 198mg; Fibre 1.6g; Sodium 86mg.

Mint and yogurt shake

Serves 2

25g/1oz/1 cup fresh mint sprigs

50g/2oz/¼ cup caster/superfine sugar

200g/7oz/scant 1 cup natural/ plain yogurt

200ml/7fl oz/scant 1 cup full-fat/ whole milk

15ml/1 tbsp lemon juice

crushed ice

icing/confectioners' sugar, to decorate

If you have mint growing in your garden, pick some for this recipe, as the fresher the mint, the better the flavour will be. The mint is infused in a sugar syrup, then left to cool before being blended to an aromatic, frothy shake with yogurt and creamy milk. The final milkshake is speckled with tiny green flecks, but if you prefer a completely smooth texture, you can strain these out.

1 Pull out four small mint sprigs and set aside. Roughly snip the remaining leaves into a small pan. Add the sugar and pour over 105ml/7 tbsp water.

2 Heat the mixture, stirring occasionally, until the sugar dissolves, then boil for 2 minutes. Remove the pan from the heat and set aside for 10 minutes to steep and cool.

3 Strain the cooled syrup through a sieve into a jug or pitcher, pressing the mint against the side of the sieve with the back of a spoon. Pour into a blender goblet.

4 Add the yogurt and milk to the goblet. Screw on the lid and blend until smooth and frothy. Add two of the reserved mint sprigs and the lemon juice and blend until the milkshake is specked with tiny green flecks.

5 Put the crushed ice in two glasses and pour over the milkshake. Dust the reserved mint sprigs with icing sugar and use to decorate the glasses. Serve.

Energy 299kcal/1272kJ; Protein 8.8g; Carbohydrate 64.5g, of which sugars 64.5g; Fat 2.7g, of which saturates 1.6g; Cholesterol 7mg; Calcium 337mg; Fibre 0g; Sodium 129mg.

Rosemary and almond cream

This concoction consists of fresh sprigs of rosemary, infused in milk, which provide a gentle fragrance and flavour that blends deliciously with the sweet ratafia biscuits.

1 Put the rosemary in a small pan. Add 150ml/¼ pint/⅔ cup of the milk and heat very gently until the milk begins to boil. Remove from the heat and leave to steep and cool for 10 minutes.

2 Remove the rosemary and pour the milk into a blender goblet. Add the ratafia biscuits. Screw on the lid and blend until smooth, then add the remaining 250ml/8fl oz/1 cup milk and blend again.

3 Scoop the ice cream into the mixture and blend. Pour into two glasses and serve immediately, decorating the top of each glass with frosted rosemary sprigs and some crumbled ratafia biscuits.

Serves 2

4 long sprigs of fresh rosemary

400ml/14fl oz/1⅔ cups milk

50g/2oz ratafia biscuits/almond macaroons or amaretti, plus extra, crumbled, to decorate

3 large scoops of vanilla ice cream

frosted rosemary, to decorate

SHAKE TIP – To make frosted rosemary, coat the sprigs in beaten egg white. Dip in caster/superfine sugar and leave to dry.

Pistachio thick-shake

Don't be put off by the presence of rice in this layered dairy-free milkshake. Blended with soya milk, pistachio nuts and non-dairy ice cream, it makes a delectable creamy blend.

1 Put the milk in a pan with the rice, sugar and lemon rind. Bring to the boil, then reduce to a simmer. Partially cover and simmer for 30 minutes, until the rice is tender. Transfer to a bowl to cool.

2 Put the nuts in a heatproof bowl and cover with boiling water. Leave to stand for 2 minutes, then drain. Rub the nuts between layers of kitchen paper to loosen the skins, then peel them away.

3 Blend the rice in a blender goblet until smooth. Put half in a bowl. Add the ice cream to the blender and blend until smooth. Pour into a separate bowl. Add the nuts, the reserved rice and the almond extract to the blender and process until finely ground. Layer the three mixtures in tall glasses. Serve with extra pistachios.

Serves 2–3

550ml/18fl oz/2½ cups soya milk

50g/2oz/generous ¼ cup pudding rice

60ml/4 tbsp caster/superfine sugar

finely grated rind of 1 lemon

75g/3oz/¾ cup shelled pistachio nuts, plus extra to decorate

300ml/10fl oz vanilla iced non-dairy dessert

5ml/1 tsp almond extract

Rosemary: Energy 400kcal/1684kJ; Protein 12.3g; Carbs 51.5g, of which sugars 39.4g; Fat 16.4g, of which saturates 10.5g; Cholesterol 39mg; Calcium 385mg; Fibre 0.4g; Sodium 236mg.
Pistachio :Energy 397kcal/1660kJ; Protein 11.4g; Carbs 47.1g, of which sugars 34.1g; Fat 18.6g, of which saturates 4.8g; Cholesterol 5mg; Calcium 154mg; Fibre 1.2g; Sodium 189mg.

Rose petal and almond milkshake

If you're lucky enough to have a mass of roses in the garden, it's well worth sacrificing a few to make this delicately scented summer shake. Thickened and flavoured with ground ratafia biscuits, this fragrant drink is the perfect way to relax on a hot lazy afternoon.

Serves 2

15g/½oz scented rose petals, washed, plus extra to decorate

300ml/½ pint/1¼ cups milk

25g/1oz ratafia biscuits/almond macaroons

ice cubes

1 Put the rose petals in a small pan with half the milk and bring just to the boil. Put the ratafia biscuits in a bowl, pour over the hot milk and leave to stand for 10 minutes.

2 Transfer the mixture to a blender goblet with the remaining milk. Screw on the lid and blend until smooth. Strain the milk into a jug or pitcher to remove any lumps of biscuit or rose petals that have not been blended properly. Chill for at least 1 hour.

3 When the milk is chilled, pour over ice cubes in two glasses and serve immediately, decorating with rose petals, if liked.

SHAKE TIP – Wash the rose petals thoroughly before you use them for cooking, to remove any chemicals or pesticides that may have been sprayed on to the flowers.

Banana and maple crunch shake

Brilliant for making quick and easy blended drinks, bananas have a natural affinity with maple syrup and pecan nuts – what a combination. It is best to serve this shake as soon as it is ready because it will not keep well. Fortunately, finishing it off in one sitting should not be too difficult.

Serves 2

2 large ripe bananas, peeled and sliced

50g/2oz/½ cup pecan nuts, plus extra to decorate

60ml/4 tbsp pure maple syrup

150ml/¼ pint/⅔ cup full-fat/whole milk

crushed ice

1 Put the bananas in a blender goblet. Screw on the lid and process until smooth. Add the nuts and blend again until well combined. The nuts must be finely ground so stop and scrape down from the sides of the goblet once or twice if necessary.

2 Add the maple syrup, then pour the milk over the banana paste and blend again until creamy.

3 Half-fill two large glasses with crushed ice and pour over the shake. Decorate with extra pecan nuts, if you like. Serve.

SHAKE TIP – For maximum flavour, it is important to use ripe bananas in this recipe.

Rose: Energy 124kcal/523kJ; Protein 5.8g; Carbohydrate 17g, of which sugars 11.5g; Fat 4.2g, of which saturates 2.4g; Cholesterol 9mg; Calcium 197mg; Fibre 0.2g; Sodium 106mg.
Banana: Energy 391kcal/1641kJ; Protein 6.2g; Carbohydrate 51.9g, of which sugars 49.2g; Fat 19.1g, of which saturates 2.4g; Cholesterol 4mg; Calcium 116mg; Fibre 2.3g; Sodium 115mg.

Passionata

Serves 2

90g/3½oz/1½ cup caster/superfine sugar

juice of 2 large oranges

juice of 1 lemon

6 ripe passion fruit, plus extra to decorate

550ml/18fl oz/2½ cups full-fat/whole milk

ice cubes

SHAKE TIP - To make the decoration, carefully quarter one passion fruit, trying to keep the seeds in place. Skewer with a cocktail stick and place across the top of the glasses.

The combination of ripe passion fruit with sweet caramel is gorgeous in this dreamy milkshake. For convenience, you can easily make the caramel syrup and combine it with the fresh passion fruit juice in advance, so it's all ready for blending with the milk. For the best results make sure you use really ripe, crinkly passion fruit.

1 Put the sugar in a small, heavy pan with 200ml/7fl oz/scant 1 cup water. Heat gently, stirring with a wooden spoon, until the sugar has dissolved.

2 Bring the mixture to the boil and cook, without stirring, for about 5 minutes until the syrup has turned to a deep golden caramel. Watch closely towards the end of the cooking time as caramel can burn very quickly.

3 When the caramel has turned deep golden, immediately lower the base of the pan into a basin of cold water to prevent it from cooking any further.

4 Carefully add the orange and lemon juice, standing back slightly as the mixture will splutter. Dry the base of the pan and return it to the heat and cook gently, stirring continuously, to make a smooth syrup. Transfer the syrup to a small heatproof bowl and set aside until it has cooled completely.

5 Halve the passion fruit and scoop the seeds into a blender goblet. Add the caramel and milk. Screw on the lid and blend until smooth and frothy.

6 Pour the mixture over ice in two glasses and serve with the passion fruit decoration, if liked (see Shake Tip).

Energy 197kcal/828kJ; Protein 5.4g; Carbohydrate 33.2g, of which sugars 33.2g; Fat 5.5g, of which saturates 3.5g; Cholesterol 19mg; Calcium 179mg; Fibre 0.8g; Sodium 67mg.

Coconut ice

Nothing beats the unadulterated flavour of freshly juiced coconut. Whizzed with ice and teamed with sharp passion fruit, it produces a milkshake that tastes indulgently good but still refreshingly natural and wholesome.

Serves 2–3

1 coconut

75ml/5 tbsp icing/confectioners' sugar

3 passion fruit

150g/5oz crushed ice

60ml/4 tbsp double/heavy cream

1 Drain the water from the coconut and reserve. Break open the coconut, remove the flesh, then peel off the brown skin. Push the coconut pieces through a juicer along with 150ml/¼ pint/⅔ cup water. Stir the sugar into the coconut juice and set aside. Halve the passion fruit and scoop the pulp into a small bowl. Set aside.

2 Put the crushed ice in a blender goblet. Screw on the lid and process until slushy. Add the juiced coconut, any drained coconut water from inside the coconut and the cream. Blitz to blend.

3 Pour the mixture into two or three tall glasses, then, using a teaspoon, spoon the passion fruit on top of the drink. Add stirrers, if you like, and serve immediately.

Deep chocolate

Only two ingredients are used in this decadently rich shake: creamy milk and chocolate. Blended together, they make the smoothest, frothiest and most chocolatey drink you will ever taste. This is definitely a treat!

Serves 2

150g/5oz good-quality chocolate

350ml/12fl oz/1½ cups full-fat/whole milk

ice cubes

chocolate curls or shavings, to decorate

1 Break the chocolate into pieces and place in a bowl set over a pan of simmering water. Add 60ml/4 tbsp of the milk and leave until the chocolate melts, stirring occasionally.

2 Remove the bowl from the heat and pour the remaining milk over the chocolate, stirring to combine. Leave to cool.

3 Pour the mixture into a blender goblet. Screw on the lid and blend until smooth and frothy. Pour into two glasses, add ice cubes and serve, topped with the chocolate decoration.

SHAKE TIP – Use dark/bittersweet chocolate with 70 per cent cocoa solids, a good-quality milk chocolate, or half of each type.

Coconut: Energy 247kcal/1041kJ; Protein 1.4g; Carbohydrate 37.1g, of which sugars 37.1g; Fat 11.4g, of which saturates 7.1g; Cholesterol 27mg; Calcium 83mg; Fibre 0.5g; Sodium 229mg.
Chocolate: Energy 463kcal/1944kJ; Protein 9.7g; Carbohydrate 55.9g, of which sugars 55.2g; Fat 24g, of which saturates 14.5g; Cholesterol 15mg; Calcium 235mg; Fibre 1.9g; Sodium 80mg.

Chocolate brownie milkshake

Serves 2

75g/3oz chocolate brownies

400ml/14fl oz/1⅔ cups full-fat/whole milk

2 scoops of vanilla ice cream

a little whipped cream

chocolate shavings or unsweetened cocoa powder, to decorate

SHAKE TIP – If you fancy treating yourself to an even more chocolatey milkshake, replace the vanilla ice cream with a chocolate or chocolate-chip variety.

For a truly indulgent flavour, use homemade chocolate brownies in this fabulously tasty milkshake, which would be ideal in place of a dessert. It is very rich and decadent, so sit back, relax and enjoy a totally luxurious moment.

1 Crumble the chocolate brownies into a blender goblet and add the milk. Screw on the lid and blend together.

2 Add the ice cream and blend until smooth and frothy.

3 Pour into two glasses and spoon over a little whipped cream. Serve immediately, sprinkled with chocolate shavings or a dusting of cocoa powder.

Energy 637kcal/2652kJ; Protein 15.4g; Carbohydrate 54.4g, of which sugars 45.5g; Fat 41g, of which saturates 18.6g; Cholesterol 28mg; Calcium 416mg; Fibre 0g; Sodium 348mg.

Cinnamon iced coffee

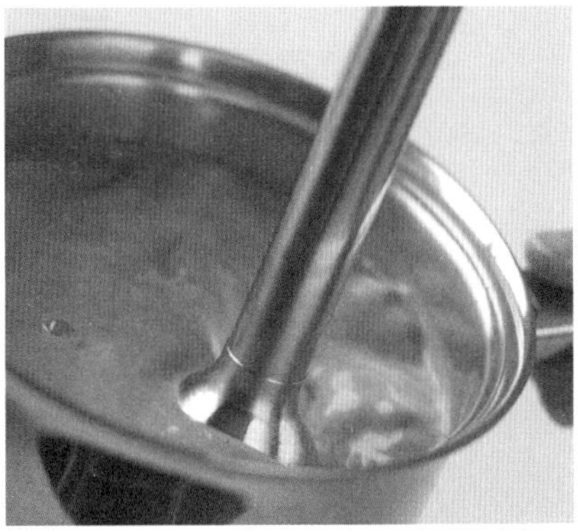

When the weather warms up, swap mugs of hot coffee for this treat of a summer cooler. Lightly flavoured with cinnamon and served icy cold, it's a smooth, relaxing drink for when you need to unwind. It's well worth keeping a pitcher of it in the fridge.

1 Put the cinnamon and 100ml/3½fl oz/ scant ½ cup of the milk in a small pan with the sugar. Bring the milk slowly to the boil, then remove from the heat and leave to cool.

2 Add the remaining milk and the coffee and whisk well, using a hand-held electric wand, until frothy. Pour into two glasses with some ice cubes and serve with cinnamon sticks for stirrers.

Serves 2

5ml/1 tsp ground cinnamon

400ml/14fl oz/1⅔ cups full-fat/whole milk

45ml/3 tbsp caster/superfine sugar

300ml/½ pint/1¼ cups strong cold espresso coffee

ice cubes

cinnamon sticks, for stirrers

SHAKE TIP – For a supper party, you could spice things up and serve these shakes with the addition of a dash of a cream-based liqueur.

Energy 218kcal/915kJ; Protein 7.1g; Carbohydrate 30.8g, of which sugars 29.9g; Fat 8.2g, of which saturates 5.1g; Cholesterol 28mg; Calcium 251mg; Fibre 0g; Sodium 88mg.

Espresso crush

Serves 2

75ml/5 tbsp ground espresso coffee

75g/3oz/scant ½ cup caster/superfine sugar

300g/11oz vanilla ice cream or vanilla iced non-dairy dessert

75ml/5 tbsp milk or soya milk

SHAKE TIP – The softened ice cream will melt quickly once you start layering it up in the glasses, so a good trick is to thoroughly chill the glasses before using them.

A fresh update on iced coffee, this creatively layered treat combines slushy frozen coffee granita with a thick vanilla ice cream layer, and is perfect for rounding off a lazy summer lunch or as a late-afternoon refresher. It's also smart enough to serve at a dinner party. The granita needs several hours in the freezer but will then keep for weeks so it is ready and waiting whenever you fancy a burst of ice-cold espresso.

1 Put the coffee in a cafetière or press pot, add 750ml/1¼ pints/3 cups boiling water and leave to infuse for 5 minutes. Plunge and pour the coffee into a shallow non-metallic freezer container. Stir in the sugar until dissolved.

2 Leave to go cold, then cover and freeze for about 2 hours or until the mixture starts to turn slushy around the edges.

3 Using a fork, break up the ice crystals, stirring them into the centre of the container. Re-freeze until the mixture is slushy around the edges again. Repeat the forking and stirring process once or twice more until the mixture is completely slushy and there is no liquid remaining. Re-freeze until ready to use.

4 Put the ice cream or iced dessert and milk in a blender goblet. Screw on the lid and process until thick and smooth.

5 To serve, spoon a little into the base of each of two glasses and sprinkle with a layer of the granita. Repeat the layering until the glasses are full. Serve immediately.

Energy 217kcal/915kJ; Protein 3.4g; Carbohydrate 39g, of which sugars 38.3g; Fat 6.3g, of which saturates 4.1g; Cholesterol 21mg; Calcium 115mg; Fibre 0g; Sodium 55mg.

Frosty fruit shake

Long after summer is over, you can still summon up the glorious flavours of the season by making this refreshing drink from frozen summer fruits. This purple, slushy, fruity delight will pep up even the darkest mornings. Revitalize yourself with this blend at any time of the day to give your body a well-deserved boost.

1 Take the frozen fruits straight from the freezer and tip them into a blender goblet. Screw on the lid and blend until finely crushed, scraping down from the sides of the goblet if necessary.

2 Add the yogurt and cream to the crushed fruit, then spoon in 30ml/2 tbsp of the sugar. Blend again until the mixture is smooth and thick. Taste and add the extra sugar if necessary. Pour into two or three glasses and serve immediately, decorated with fruit.

Serves 2–3

250g/9oz/2 cups frozen summer fruits, plus extra to decorate

200g/7oz/scant 1 cup natural/plain yogurt

45ml/3 tbsp double/heavy cream

30–45ml/2–3 tbsp caster/superfine sugar

SHAKE TIP – This drink takes only moments to whizz up and you can use any mixture of fruits, whether you've grown your own berries or bought them frozen in bags.

Energy 174kcal/726kJ; Protein 4.4g; Carbohydrate 20.7g, of which sugars 20.7g; Fat 8.8g, of which saturates 5.3g; Cholesterol 21mg; Calcium 153mg; Fibre 0.9g; Sodium 64mg.

Thyme-scented plum slush

Serves 2–3

400g/14oz red plums
30–45ml/2–3 tbsp clear honey
15ml/1 tbsp chopped fresh lemon thyme, plus extra thyme sprigs, to decorate
100g/3¾oz crushed ice

SHAKE TIP – Dark, purplish-red plums, with their almost violet bloom and sweet, intense flavour, juice well and make some of the most tempting and vibrant fruit drinks.

Make this drink in the early autumn when plums are at their best. Their silky smooth flesh blends down to produce the most wonderfully textured slush, while delicately scented lemon thyme and honey complement the flavour perfectly. This luxurious juice is easy to make and has an irresistible fragrance that is at once warming and refreshing.

1 Using a sharp knife, halve and pit the plums and put them in a blender goblet. Add 30ml/2 tbsp of the honey and the lemon thyme. Screw on the lid and blitz until smooth, scraping down from the sides of the goblet if necessary.

2 Add the ice and blend until slushy. Taste for sweetness, adding a little more honey if necessary. Pour into two or three glasses and serve immediately, decorated with a sprig of thyme.

Energy 77kcal/330kJ; Protein 0.8g; Carbohydrate 19.4g, of which sugars 19.4g; Fat 0.1g, of which saturates 0g; Cholesterol 0mg; Calcium 18mg; Fibre 2.1g; Sodium 4mg.

Berry blend slush

Make the syrup for this sweet, semi-frozen treat and freeze it for an hour or two, ready to blend to a slushy consistency.

Serves 2

2 oranges

250g/9oz/2¼ cups blueberries

50g/2oz/4 tbsp caster/superfine sugar

1 Cut away the majority of the skin from the oranges, then cut the flesh into 8–10 chunky wedges of roughly the same size. Reserve a few blueberries for decoration, then push the rest through a juicer, alternating them with the orange wedges.

2 Add the sugar and 300ml/½ pint/1¼ cups cold water to the juice and stir until the sugar has dissolved. Pour into a shallow, non-metallic freezer container and freeze for 1–2 hours or until the juice is beginning to freeze all over.

3 Use a fork to break up any solid areas and tip into a blender goblet. Screw on the lid and blend until smooth and slushy. Spoon into two glasses and serve, topped with blueberries.

Rainbow crush

Brightly coloured layers of pure fruit juice give this crush extra child-appeal. Check the sweetness of each juice before layering up the fruits, stirring in a little sugar if necessary.

Serves 2

4 kiwi fruit

½ small pineapple

130g/4½oz/generous 1 cup strawberries

1 Peel the kiwi fruit. Cut away the skin from the pineapple, then halve and remove the core. Roughly chop the pineapple flesh. Put the pineapple in a blender goblet and add 30ml/2 tbsp water. Screw on the lid and process to a smooth purée, scraping the mixture down from the sides if necessary. Tip into a bowl.

2 Add the kiwi fruit to the blender and blend until smooth. Tip into a separate bowl. Finally, blend the strawberries until smooth.

3 Pour the strawberry purée into two tall glasses. Carefully spoon in the kiwi fruit purée to form a separate layer, then spoon over the pineapple purée. Serve with spoons or thick straws.

SHAKE TIP – Strawberry, kiwi fruit and pineapple provide plenty of colour contrast but you can use almost any other fruits that blend to a fairly thick consistency, and create your own rainbow.

Berry: Energy 150kcal/637kJ; Protein 2g; Carbohydrate 37.6g, of which sugars 34.3g; Fat 0.1g, of which saturates 0g; Cholesterol 0mg; Calcium 56mg; Fibre 3.4g; Sodium 6mg..

Rainbow: Energy 78kcal/332kJ; Protein 1.5g; Carbohydrate 17.8g, of which sugars 17.6g; Fat 0.6g, of which saturates 0g; Cholesterol 0mg; Calcium 39mg; Fibre 2.8g; Sodium 7mg.

Cranberry, cinnamon and ginger spritz

Serves 4

600ml/1 pint/2½ cups chilled cranberry juice

150ml/¼ pint/⅔ cup clear apple juice

4 cinnamon sticks

about 400ml/14fl oz/1⅔ cups chilled ginger ale

a few fresh or frozen cranberries, to decorate

SHAKE TIP – As an alternative decoration, thread cranberries on to cocktail sticks and add one to each glass instead of a cinnamon stick.

Partially freezing fruit juice gives it a wonderfully slushy texture that is very refreshing, and it also tones down its sweetness. The combination of cranberry and apple juice contributes a tart, clean flavour that's very moreish.

1 Pour the cranberry juice into a shallow, non-metallic freezer container and freeze for 2 hours or until a thick layer of ice crystals forms around the edges.

2 Mash with a fork to break up the ice, then return the mixture to the freezer for a further 2–3 hours, until almost solid.

3 Pour the apple juice into a small pan, add two cinnamon sticks and bring to just below boiling point. Pour into a jug or pitcher and leave to cool, then remove the cinnamon sticks and set aside with the others. Chill the juice until it is very cold.

4 Spoon the cranberry ice into a blender goblet. Add the apple juice, screw on the lid and blend until slushy.

5 Pile into four cocktail glasses, top up with ginger ale and decorate with the fresh or frozen cranberries. Pop a long cinnamon stick into each glass to use as a swizzle stick.

Energy 86kcal/370kJ; Protein 0.2g; Carbohydrate 22.5g, of which sugars 22.5g; Fat 0.2g, of which saturates 0g; Cholesterol 0mg; Calcium 13mg; Fibre 0g; Sodium 4mg.

Strawberry and apple slush

Serves 2

300g/11oz/2½ cups ripe strawberries

2 small, crisp eating apples

10ml/2 tsp vanilla syrup

crushed ice

SHAKE TIP – Vanilla syrup can be bought in bottles from supermarkets and delicatessens. As a lower-sugar alternative, you could add a few drops of vanilla extract.

Sweet, juicy strawberries make wonderfully fragrant juices, especially when they are grown outside in the summer. The juice has an almost perfect consistency that's not too thick and not too thin. The addition of apple juice and just a hint of vanilla creates a tantalizing, fruity treat that's ideal when you want to spend a lazy summer afternoon in the garden.

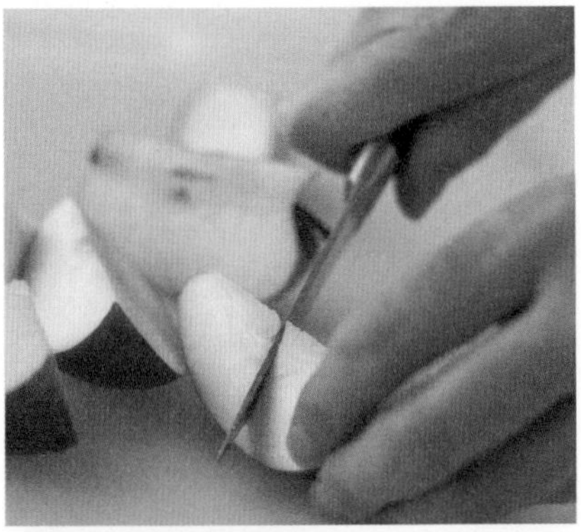

1 Pick out a couple of the prettiest strawberries and reserve for the decoration. Hull the remaining strawberries and roughly chop the apples into large chunks. Push the fruits through a juicer, then stir in the vanilla syrup.

2 Half-fill two tall glasses with crushed ice. Add straws or stirrers and pour over the juice. Decorate with the reserved strawberries (slicing them, if you like) and serve immediately.

Energy 78kcal/331kJ; Protein 1.4g; Carbohydrate 18.8g, of which sugars 18.8g; Fat 0.2g, of which saturates 0g; Cholesterol 0mg; Calcium 28mg; Fibre 2.7g; Sodium 24mg.

Cool as a currant

Serves 2

125g/4¼oz/generous 1 cup blackcurrants, plus extra to decorate

60ml/4 tbsp light muscovado/brown sugar

a good pinch of mixed/apple pie spice (optional)

crushed ice

NUTRIENT NOTE – Tiny, glossy blackcurrants are a virtual powerhouse of nutrients, being packed with vitamins C and E, as well as essential iron, calcium and magnesium.

Whizzed in a blender with crushed ice, blackcurrants make a drink so thick and slushy that you might want to serve it with long spoons so that you can scoop up every last drop.

1 Put the blackcurrants and sugar in a pan. Add the mixed spice, if using, and pour in 100ml/3½fl oz/scant ½ cup water. Bring to the boil and cook for 2–3 minutes until the blackcurrants are completely soft.

2 Strain the mixture into a bowl, pressing to extract as much juice as possible. Leave to stand until it is completely cold.

3 Put the crushed ice in a blender goblet with the cooled juice. Screw on the lid and blend for about 1 minute, until slushy. Pour into two glasses, decorate with blackcurrants and serve.

Energy 136kcal/580kJ; Protein 0.7g; Carbohydrate 35.5g, of which sugars 35.5g; Fat 0g, of which saturates 0g; Cholesterol 0mg; Calcium 54mg; Fibre 2.3g; Sodium 4mg..

Strawberries and cream

Real strawberries and cream are sublime together when fresh strawberries are at their best, and the same goes for this delectable drink. Use small, vibrantly red and thoroughly ripe fruit. Frozen whole, they serve as flavour-packed ice cubes that will chill the drink.

Serves 2

275g/10oz/2½ cups small strawberries

15ml/1 tbsp lemon juice

5ml/1 tsp vanilla sugar

cream soda

1 Hull the strawberries. Freeze about 130g/4½oz/generous 1 cup of the smallest ones for 1 hour or until firm. Process the remainder in a blender goblet with the lemon juice and sugar until smooth, scraping down from the sides if necessary.

2 Divide the frozen strawberries between two tall glasses and pour in the strawberry purée. Top up with cream soda and serve immediately with long-handled spoons so your guests can scoop out the frozen strawberries once they have thawed slightly.

SHAKE TIP – To make vanilla sugar, fill a jar with caster/superfine sugar and press a whole vanilla pod/bean into the middle. Seal and leave for 2–3 weeks before using.

Apple refresher

Here, sweet, ripe apples are juiced and then frozen until slushy. Served with additional apples and topped up with sparkling water, this drink couldn't be simpler.

Serves 2

6 large red eating apples

10ml/2 tsp lemon juice

a little clear honey (optional)

sparkling mineral water

1 Reserve one of the apples. Quarter, core and finely chop the remainder. Juice the pieces and stir in the lemon juice. Check for sweetness, adding honey, if using. (The flavour will be less sweet once frozen.) Pour into a shallow, non-metallic freezer container, cover and freeze until slush has formed around the edges.

2 Using a fork, break up the frozen apple juice, pushing it into the middle of the container. Re-freeze for 1 hour or until slushy all over. Again, break up the mixture with a fork.

3 Quarter and core the remaining apple and cut into thin slices. Spoon the slush into two glasses until two-thirds full, then tuck the slices down the sides. Top up with sparkling water to serve.

SHAKE TIP – Green and red apples produce quite different flavours in juices. Red apples are better for this recipe because the colour is pretty and the flavour light and fragrant. Crisp, green apples will give a sweeter, tangier and denser flavour.

Strawberries: Energy 45kcal/189kJ; Protein 1.1g; Carbohydrate 10.4g, of which sugars 10.4g; Fat 0.2g, of which saturates 0g; Cholesterol 0mg; Calcium 23mg; Fibre 1.5g; Sodium 9mg.

Apple: Energy 71kcal/307kJ; Protein 0.7g; Carbohydrate 18.1g, of which sugars 18.1g; Fat 0.2g, of which saturates 0g; Cholesterol 0mg; Calcium 9mg; Fibre 3.2g; Sodium 4mg.

Super sorbet fizz

Freshly blended pineapple and lemon sorbet, topped up with ginger ale, makes a tastebud-tingling drink. It's perfect after a summer lunch as a light alternative to more conventional desserts, or one to whizz up and chill out with whenever the mood takes you.

1 Mix the sugar with the lemon juice in a small bowl and leave to stand for about 5 minutes until it turns syrupy.

2 Remove the pineapple skin and core and cut the flesh into chunks. Put these in a blender goblet with the ginger. Screw on the lid and whizz until smooth, scraping down from the sides if necessary.

3 Add the sorbet and blend briefly until smooth. Spoon the syrup into four short glasses, then pour in the pineapple mixture. Decorate the sides of the glasses with the pineapple and lemon slices. Top up with ginger ale and serve immediately.

Serves 4

30ml/2 tbsp dark muscovado/ brown sugar

15ml/1 tbsp lemon juice

½ pineapple

1 piece of preserved stem ginger, roughly chopped

200ml/7fl oz/scant 1 cup lemon sorbet, slightly softened

ginger ale, chilled

wafer-thin pineapple and lemon slices, to decorate

Energy 126kcal/539kJ; Protein 0.8g; Carbohydrate 32.5g, of which sugars 32.5g; Fat 0.2g, of which saturates 0g; Cholesterol 0mg; Calcium 19mg; Fibre 0.9g; Sodium 11mg.

Lemon float

Serves 2

6 lemons, plus wafer-thin lemon slices, to decorate

200g/7oz/1 cup caster/ superfine sugar

4 scoops of vanilla ice cream

soda water/club soda

SHAKE TIP – The lemonade can be stored in the fridge for up to 2 weeks, so it is well worth making a double batch.

Old-fashioned lemonade made with freshly squeezed lemons is a far cry from the carbonated, synthetic commercial varieties. Served with generous scoops of ice cream and soda water, it makes the ultimate refreshing dessert drink.

1 Grate the rind from the lemons, then squeeze out the juice. Put the rind in a bowl with the sugar and pour over 600ml/1 pint/2½ cups boiling water. Stir until the sugar dissolves, then leave to cool.

2 Stir in the lemon juice. Strain into a jug or pitcher and chill for several hours.

3 Put a scoop of ice cream in each of two glasses, then half-fill with the lemonade and decorate with lemon slices. Top up with soda water, add another scoop of ice cream and serve.

Energy 520kcal/2182kJ; Protein 6.1g; Carbohydrate 77.5g, of which sugars 77.3g; Fat 22.7g, of which saturates 13.6g; Cholesterol 0mg; Calcium 177mg; Fibre 0g; Sodium 93mg.

Iced mango lassi

Serves 3–4

175g/6oz/scant 1 cup caster/superfine sugar

150ml/¼ pint/⅔ cup water

2 lemons

500ml/17fl oz/generous 2 cups Greek/strained plain yogurt

350ml/12fl oz/1½ cups mango juice

ice cubes (optional)

fresh mint sprigs and mango wedges, to decorate

SHAKE TIP – You could also make the yogurt ice in an ice-cream machine, if you have one. To do so, make the syrup and chill it, stir in the lemon rind and juice, then pour the liquid into an ice-cream machine instead of the freezer container and churn according to the manufacturer's instructions.

Based on a traditional Indian drink, this is perfect for any occasion: served with spicy food at dinner, at long, hot garden parties, or as a welcome cooler at any time of day. The yogurt ice that forms the basis of this drink is a useful recipe to add to your repertoire because it is much lighter and healthier than classic ice creams.

1 To make the yogurt ice, put the sugar and water in a pan and heat gently, stirring occasionally, until the sugar has dissolved. Pour the syrup into a jug or pitcher. Leave to cool, then chill until very cold.

2 Grate the rind from the lemons and then squeeze out the juice. Add the rind and juice to the chilled syrup and stir well to mix.

3 Pour the syrup mixture into a shallow, non-metallic freezer container and freeze for a couple of hours or until thickened. Beat in the yogurt and return to the freezer until the mixture is thick enough to scoop.

4 To serve the drinks, briefly process the mango juice with about 10 small scoops of yogurt ice in a blender goblet, until the mixture is just smooth.

5 Pour equal portions of the mixture into your glasses and add the ice cubes, if using. Top each drink with another scoop of the yogurt ice and decorate with mint sprigs and mango wedges. Serve immediately.

Energy 366kcal/1546kJ; Protein 8.8g; Carbohydrate 60.6g, of which sugars 60.3g; Fat 12.9g, of which saturates 6.6g; Cholesterol 0mg; Calcium 221mg; Fibre 2.3g; Sodium 93mg.

Iced pear aniseed

Serves 2–3

30ml/2 tbsp aniseeds, crushed

30ml/2 tbsp caster/
superfine sugar

3–4 soft, ripe pears

10ml/2 tsp lemon juice

crushed ice

SHAKE TIPS

- For a great-tasting juice that really packs a punch, make sure you use fresh, sweet pears as underripe ones will inevitably result in a disappointing and almost bland juice.

– It is also important to use fresh and aromatic aniseed. Like all herbs and spices, aniseed loses its flavour quickly and, when it turns stale, it lacks flavour and has a slightly musty aroma.

Aniseed is a spice widely used in cooking, not only in sweet and savoury dishes but as the dominant flavour in many alcoholic drinks like pastis, ouzo and raki. If these flavours appeal to you – without the alcohol – you'll love this deliciously spicy pear-based iced infusion.

1 Put the crushed aniseeds in a small pan with the sugar and 100ml/3½fl oz/scant ½ cup water. Heat very gently, stirring until the sugar has dissolved. Bring to the boil and boil for 1 minute. Remove from the heat and leave to cool.

2 Quarter and core the pears. Keeping some wedges to add to the glasses, press the pears through a juicer. Add the lemon juice. Strain the aniseed syrup into the pear juice and chill until ready to serve. Pour over crushed ice in two or three glasses.

Energy 99kcal/422kJ; Protein 0.5g; Carbohydrate 25.4g, of which sugars 25.4g; Fat 0.2g, of which saturates 0g; Cholesterol 0mg; Calcium 22mg; Fibre 3.3g; Sodium 5mg.

Pineapple and yogurt ice

Serves 2

25g/1oz fresh basil, plus extra sprigs, to decorate

1 pineapple

4 large scoops of vanilla-, lemon- or orange-flavoured yogurt ice

icing/confectioners' sugar, for dusting

SHAKE TIP – Fresh mint makes an equally refreshing alternative to basil if you have plenty growing in the garden, or try other soft-leaved herbs, such as lemon balm.

Yogurt ice can be bought in several flavours, or you can make your own – see p260 and p265. It is perfect in summer drinks as a lighter alternative to ice cream. Use a sweet, juicy pineapple and fresh, pungent basil to add vibrant colour and exotic flavour to this refreshing iced drink.

1 Remove the basil leaves from the stems and tear them into small pieces with your fingers.

2 Cut away the skin from the pineapple, then halve and remove the core. Chop the flesh into chunks. Push the pineapple through a juicer with the basil. Chill the mixture until ready to serve.

3 Pour the juice into two glasses and add two scoops of yogurt ice to each. Decorate with basil sprigs and dust with icing sugar.

Energy 353kcal/1488kJ; Protein 5.7g; Carbohydrate 58.5g, of which sugars 57.3g; Fat 12.3g, of which saturates 7.2g; Cholesterol 11mg; Calcium 162mg; Fibre 3.6g; Sodium 99mg.

Fire and ice

Tickle your tastebuds with this unconventional frozen yogurt drink, which is flavoured with fresh orange juice and specks of fresh red chilli. It's great on a hot summer's day, after lunch or any other time when you're in need of a refreshing boost. If you've time and the inclination, add an alcoholic kick to the drink by drizzling each glass with a splash of orange-flavoured liqueur before serving.

Serves 2

90g/3½oz/½ cup caster/superfine sugar

1 lemon

300ml/½ pint/1¼ cups freshly squeezed orange juice

200g/7oz/scant 1 cup Greek/strained plain yogurt

1 fresh red chilli, seeded and finely chopped

60ml/4 tbsp Cointreau or other orange-flavoured liqueur (optional)

orange slices and extra fresh chillies, split in half lengthways, to decorate

1 Put the sugar in a pan with 100ml/3½fl oz/scant ½ cup water and heat gently, stirring with a wooden spoon until the sugar has dissolved. Pour into a shallow non-metallic freezer container and leave to cool.

2 Finely grate the rind of the lemon, then squeeze the juice using a citrus juicer. Add the lemon rind and juice and 100ml/3½fl oz/scant ½ cup of the orange juice to the container with the sugar syrup. Freeze for 2 hours or until a band of ice has formed around the edges.

3 Turn into a bowl and add the yogurt and chopped chilli. Whisk until thick. Freeze for 1–2 hours until almost solid. Alternatively, you could use an ice-cream machine, if you have one. To do so, pour the chilled lemon and sugar syrup into the machine, then add the yogurt and chilli and churn according to the manufacturer's instructions.

4 To serve, scoop the frozen yogurt into a blender goblet and add the remaining orange juice. Process the mixture until it's very thick and smooth.

5 Pour into two tall glasses and drizzle with a little orange-flavoured liqueur, if using. Decorate with orange slices and split fresh red chillies, then serve.

SHAKE TIP – Don't worry if you forget to remove the chilli yogurt from the freezer before it has frozen solid. Leave it at room temperature for a while to soften or simply heat it briefly in a microwave.

Energy 234kcal/989kJ; Protein 5.4g; Carbohydrate 41.6g, of which sugars 41.6g; Fat 7g, of which saturates 3.5g; Cholesterol 0mg; Calcium 131mg; Fibre 0.1g; Sodium 60mg.

Index

Acknowledgements

Published by Lorenz Books
an imprint of Anness Publishing Ltd
info@anness.com; www.lorenzbooks.com

 A CIP catalogue record for this book is available from the British Library.

Publisher: Joanna Lorenz
Editorial and design: Lucy Doncaster
Recipe contributors: Sara Lewis, Joanna Farrow, Suzannah Olivier
Photographers: Gus Filgate, William Shaw, Craig Robertson
Nutritional consultant: Clare Emery
Index: Marie Lorimer
Production controller: Ben Worley
With many thanks to the other contributors, photographers and stylists.

Some recipes have been previously published in *The Green Juice Book, Superfood Breakfasts,* and *Juicing, Smoothies and Blended Drinks.*

PUBLISHER'S NOTE
Although the advice and information in this book are believed to be accurate and true at the time of going to press, neither the authors nor the publisher can accept any legal responsibility or liability for any errors or omissions that may have been made, nor for any inaccuracies, nor for any loss, harm or injury that comes about from following instructions or advice in this book. The book is not intended as a substitute for professional health advice.

KITCHEN NOTES
For all recipes, quantities are given in both metric, imperial measures and where appropriate, measures are also given in standard spoons and cups. Follow one set of measures, but not a mixture, because they are not interchangeable. Standard spoon and cup measures are level. 1 tsp = 5ml, 1 tbsp = 15ml, 1 cup = 250ml/8fl oz. Australian standard tablespoons are 20ml; Australian readers should use 3 tsp in place of 1 tbsp for measuring small quantities. American pints are 16fl oz/2 cups; American readers should use 20fl oz/2.5 cups in place of 1 pint when measuring liquids. Garnishes are optional and not included in the nutritional analysis. Nutritional analysis is based on the whole quantity, not per serving, since glass sizes vary.